Endorsements

D1547729

"My faith was challenged and inspired as I read *There Is No Normal: Finding Hope in the Dailyness of Grief,* the very gripping book by my long-time friend, Anne Alexander, in which she shares the shocking story of her husband's very unexpected death. Anne, who was age 33 at the time, is suddenly facing life without her loving companion and with two small children at her side. She takes us on a long and difficult trek from shock, heartbreak, despair, and anger to trust in the goodness and faithfulness of God that leads her to peace that passes all understanding. I strongly encourage you to read this powerful book and walk with Anne on an amazing journey of healing and restoration. This book is a must-read for anyone dealing with grief."

– Doug Carter, Sr. Vice President, EQUIP

"As a young pastor of a new church in Atlanta, GA in 1985, I had only officiated one other funeral when Anne's husband passed away. Mike and I were the same age, 37. He was our only adult Sunday School teacher, and his sudden death left an indelible imprint on our small congregation. Over the past thirty-two years, Anne's grief journey has taken her through significant unfamiliar territory, but her deeply-rooted faith has been the determining factor in weathering the biggest storm of her life. As she gives the reader glimpses into the window of her heart, Anne's story gives hope. Her storytelling ability is captivating and undeniable. I expected something honest and inspirational and challenging, with a bit of humor sprinkled throughout—and I was not disappointed."

**– Randy Pope, Founding Pastor and Lead Teacher,
Perimeter Church, Johns Creek, GA**

"No one escapes life without pain. But there is always hope, and that is exactly what Anne Alexander delivers in her powerfully written book, *There Is No Normal: Finding Hope in the Dailyness of Grief.* As a mom of two young children, she experienced the sudden death of her 37-year-old husband. Anne doesn't depict her grief through the lens of spiritual rose-colored glasses. Instead, her story paints a clear picture of the deep sorrow she felt, and how she met the challenge to find hope—rather than get stuck in the quagmire of grief. Her presentation is not only thought-provoking, it is inspiring and gives hope.

I know Anne, and her story. I believe you or someone you love will greatly benefit from it."

– Dan Reiland, Executive Pastor,
12Stone Church, Atlanta GA

"We will never know the "why" to some of our questions here on earth. All of us must live without certainty, but we don't have to live with angst. My long-time friend and colleague, Anne Alexander, shares glimpses into how she managed her conflicted heart when her whole world came crashing down. *There Is No Normal: Finding Peace in the Dailyness of Grief* will give hurting hearts practical help and more importantly, hope to face tomorrow."

– Dr. Tim Elmore, Founder and President of Growing Leaders

"Christ followers are simply sojourners whose real home is heaven. Hopefully, as we age, we grow in wisdom for service in Christ's Kingdom. God called Anne to widowhood at a younger age than most. I entered Anne's life soon after her husband Mike left it. I watched her grow in wisdom. I watched as she clung with determination and resolve to the Source of wisdom in many, many trials. God never failed her. The poets David and Isaiah are two Bible writers she likes to reference. Like them, she found comfort in pouring out her heart in insightful poetry. Her testimony of God's faithfulness exemplifies the truth that God is the "husband" of widows. "*Father of the fatherless and protector of widows is God in his holy habitation*" (Psalm 68:5).

While this book seems to be a memoir, it is actually a life lesson from Anne in how to *walk the talk*. Remember, Anne is a teacher. She was my Bible teacher as well as being my friend. She is transparent, honest and yes, sometimes painfully truthful. She reveals the depth of her love and trust in God in this testimony of the God who walked it all with her.

Her insights will encourage anyone grieving and will guide those who support hurting persons. I cannot think of a better "sympathy card" than the encouragement provided in this book."

– Carolyn Benoit

"In her book *There Is No Normal: Finding Hope in the Dailyness of Grief*, Anne Alexander has given us more than *hope* that can be found along the dark pathway of grief, but she also has provided us with the inspiration, instruction and most of all, the example needed to navigate the pain and heartache of loss. Anne and I have been friends for 38 years and our husbands were good friends until Jesus took each of them home earlier than either of us wanted. Since Mike's death preceded my husband's death by ten years, Anne pioneered for me the lessons that grief has to teach. She was my model for widowhood and continues to be that model for all those within her sphere of influence. Thankfully, Anne now has highlighted those lessons in her new book, enabling her godly pattern of handling loss to be communicated to so many more."

– **Sally Gresham, Founder,** *Divine Providence Training Center,* **Pastor Training, Kenya**

THERE IS NO
Normal

There Is No Normal

FINDING HOPE IN THE DAILYNESS OF GRIEF

ANNE ALEXANDER

©2018 Dust Jacket Press
There is No Normal: Finding Hope in the Dailyness of Grief" / Anne Alexander

ISBN: 978-1-947671-18-8

Dust Jacket Press
P.O. Box 721243
Oklahoma City, OK73172
www.dustjacket.com

Dust Jacket logos are registered trademarks of Dust Jacket Press, Inc.

Cover & Interior Design: D.E. West / ZAQ Designs - Dust Jacket Creative Services

Printed in the United States of America

www.dustjacket.com

DEDICATION

To my children, their spouses, and my grandchildren,

I pray that your love for one another continues to grow immeasurably throughout your lives, and may your love for Jesus shine brightly to everyone that crosses your paths. May you love the Lord *"with all your heart, and with all your soul, and with all your mind"* (Matthew 22:37). Your spiritual heritage is rich, and I'm confident that the Lord will use each one of you to further His Kingdom, as you exercise your unique gifts.

With all my love, Mom & Grandma

TABLE OF CONTENTS

Dedication xi

1. In the Blink of an Eye... 1

2. Daddy's with Jesus. Why Is Everybody Crying? 13

3. One Funeral Down . . . and One to Go.................... 25

4. Home Sweet Home... 39

5. The Many Faces of Grief 47

6. Never-Ending Daily Adjustments............................. 61

7. Can God Be Trusted? Really?.................................... 69

8. Keep Eternity's Perspective 77

9. Take One Day at a Time... 91

10. Find at Least One Blessing Each Day 103

11. One-Anothering.. 111

12. The Making of Gold... 119

13. Peace That Passes All Understanding 121

14. God Is Always Working Behind the Scenes 129

About the Author... 137

Chapter One

In the Blink of an Eye

*"I would rather have thirty minutes of wonderful
than a lifetime of nothing special."*
– Shelby, Steel Magnolias

In the blink of an eye, life can change dramatically
. . . for better or for worse. As quick as it takes to
say, "I do," we transition from a state of singleness to being
married. One ring from our cell phone and instantly we
transition from being unemployed to landing our dream
job. One moment we feel perfectly healthy, but in a mil-
lisecond a medical test confirms our worst nightmare. On
any given day or night, life as we know it can change in the
blink of an eye.

When my husband came home from work one Friday
night, he had some exciting news. He had signed up five
new clients that day. Not a bad day's work—especially for a
brand-new company—so he wanted to celebrate! We man-

aged to find a sitter, which was an amazing feat on a Friday night, and we kissed our kids goodnight. We were off to enjoy dinner and a movie.

Mike told me about his new clients and the web of connections that led them to find "Alexander and Associates." We had lived in the Atlanta area for seven years, and Mike had established a significant network of contacts. At dinner, he started to launch off into his "financial/accountant lingo" (percentages of this and that, etc.), but I interrupted him, saying, "Spare me the details." We both laughed and changed the subject of conversation! We had established years ago that he was the "numbers guy" and I was the "word girl." So far, our complementary skills had worked out just fine in our marriage!

We arrived at the theater just in time to see the beginning of the 1985 movie, *Places in the Heart,* starring Sally Field as Edna Spalding. Early in the movie, Edna experienced the reality of just how quickly life can change. Her husband, the local sheriff, was tragically killed in a drive-by shooting. In the blink of an eye her world was turned upside down!

Following the funeral, a neighbor offered to keep Edna's two young boys for a few hours, so she could get some rest. The big screen managed to capture the emotional moment when Edna walked into her house—her very empty, quiet house. The silence was deafening. She was still too numb to feel much of anything, except for the overriding sense of being all alone. Just two short days ago, this house was filled with boisterous laughter during wrestling matches between the boys and their dad. But in the blink of an eye, now it was strangely quiet—no laughter, no wrestling, no Daddy.

The idea of "resting" was impossible for Edna. How could she? There were too many things to think about—the boys, their future, the farm, the monthly bills, the mortgage, the car, the taxes. And then another thought hit her like a ton of bricks—she had to find a job. She hadn't worked outside of her home since their first son was born. What would she do? How could they ever make it?

It didn't take long for Edna's emotions to change from sorrow and grief to anger. She was angry that her husband died—and that she was still alive. She was angry that she was now a single parent . . . and penniless in the midst of the Great Depression. It was a powerful scene. In fact, it was so compelling I sat in the theater and tried to imagine how that would feel. I'm usually not emotional at movies, but this particular storyline grabbed my heart. In that agonizing moment, I hurt for her. How horrible it would be to have a husband one minute and suddenly lose him forever—with two small children to raise, alone. Like Edna, the thought of bearing the weight of all that responsibility was inconceivable to me.

Before I could dwell on that thought for very long, however, Edna was faced with a new dilemma. A week or so had gone by when the younger son showed a defiant and disrespectful attitude toward his mother. Up until now, her husband had been the disciplinarian, so Edna was in a quandary about what to do. After all, his father had just died. Maybe she should cut him some slack. On the other hand, this might be a defining moment that would set the tone for future confrontations.

She was confident of one thing, however. She knew that if his father was still alive, their son would receive "a big whoopin" for his attitude and behavior. After a few minutes of pondering, she decided that her son's blatant defiance warranted some discipline. As they were on their way to get "a switch" from the backyard, her face clearly showed anxiety about having to administer his punishment.

It was at this point that my husband chuckled and nudged my elbow, whispering mischievously, "You wouldn't have such a hard time doing that!" We both snickered. You see, our parental agreement was that whichever parent was "at the scene of the crime" was the one who handled the discipline.

After his wisecrack, Mike grabbed another handful of popcorn. While there was still a smile on my face, he cleared his throat with just one small "uh-umm." We were sharing a big bucket of popcorn, so I assumed he was clearing a popcorn hull from his throat. However, instead of grabbing another handful of popcorn, his whole body shivered, and his head went back on the theater seat. I thought he was still just joking around. His quick wit kept us laughing a lot. But when I reached for another handful of popcorn, I realized he hadn't moved again—at all. He obviously wasn't joking around now because the only time Mike was motionless was when he was asleep. In his "awake" hours, he had enough energy for an entire roomful of people. Something was wrong. I turned to the strangers sitting directly behind us in the theater and asked, "Could you get some help? I think my husband is ill."

Within minutes, a doctor came from the movie theater next to ours. We lived in a small town, and the guy behind the snack counter had seen one of the local doctors come in, so he knew there was a doctor in the house.

Had I not been there, I never would have believed that professional help could have arrived so quickly. The doctor pulled my husband into the aisle and immediately started to perform CPR on him. Two nurses that were seated nearby also came to assist the doctor (like I said, it was a small town). We were sitting in the back of the theater, so only the last few rows of people in our section were distracted with the flurry of activity. The rest of the movie patrons were undisturbed as the movie reel kept rolling.

FULL-BLOWN PANDEMONIUM

When the EMT's arrived, however, the theater manager decided to evacuate the theater. Now try to imagine the scenario. Twenty minutes into the movie, you see the screen go black, the house lights come on, and everyone is being corralled out the front exit doors . . . with no explanation.

When the mass exodus began, there was much confusion—as you can well imagine. Understandably, the crowd wanted some answers. They were clearly annoyed about this unexplained interruption. Some teenagers were yelling, "What do you mean we have to leave? The movie just got started!" Older people were asking if (and when) they'd get their money back . . . and how? Mostly, though, faces were filled with questions and blank stares. Why had the movie stopped? Why did they have to leave? What was going on?

The confusion quickly escalated to anger—that is, until those patrons being led out of the theater saw a man on the floor in the aisle, receiving CPR. Then screams of fear and panic quickly replaced the anger. It was Friday night and the theater was full. In the blink of an eye, full-blown pandemonium broke out.

ANGELS IN DISGUISE

In the midst of all the shrieking and chaos, the EMT's directed me to move to the front of the theater. It still didn't cross my mind that anything was seriously wrong. Mike was fine at dinner. He was chowing down his food like usual. He hadn't mentioned not feeling well. After all, it was his idea to go to dinner and a movie to celebrate his new clients. Why would he suggest that if he didn't feel well? Plus, just a few minutes earlier we had laughed together at his wisecrack!

Before I moved to the front of the theater, I asked those same people that were sitting behind us if they would mind calling our neighbors for me, so they could let our babysitter know we would be home later than we had planned. I know it's hard for some of you to imagine, but thirty plus years ago, there were no cell phones. Nor did they have defibrillators in public places. I gave those strangers our neighbor's phone number and said, "Please tell them we'll be home soon." They graciously agreed to call our neighbors. I never saw them again. To this day, I do not know who they were, but they helped me twice on that Friday night in February 1985 . . . and I am forever grateful.

One never knows how you will react in a time of crisis—until you are in one. At the height of the pandemonium, I remember closing my eyes and silently praying. I knew that God was the *only* One who could fix whatever was wrong. Silently, I prayed, "Lord, I don't know what's wrong, but please give the Dr. and the paramedics Your wisdom as they work on Mike. You are the only One who can heal whatever is wrong." When the EMT's asked me to move to the front of the theater, it was empty except for an older couple that was sitting in the front center section.

When the woman saw me walking toward the front, she got up and met me in the aisle. I was immediately drawn to the kindness in her eyes. She gently took my hand and asked if they could drive me to the hospital. She explained they had a married daughter about my age. Then she said, "If something like this happened to her, we would hope someone would stay with her."

Before I answered her, I turned around to see what the paramedics were doing with Mike. They had already left—without me! I had remained calm throughout all the pandemonium, but this made me mad. Why didn't they tell me they were leaving? I was ignorant about the medical protocol in this situation, but at the very least I felt like someone should have told me they were leaving!

The Lord graciously provided this sweet couple—forever known in my mind as the "angels in disguise." At their insistence, I rode with them to the hospital. On the way, they asked me questions like where we lived, how long had we been in town, where my husband worked, etc. The wife asked if we had children. "Yes," I answered. "We have a little boy who is eight and a little girl that just turned four." Two of their grandchildren were the same ages. In hindsight, it was way out of character for me to get into a car with total strangers and answer a battery of questions—but these circumstances also were "unknown territory" for me. Sometimes "ignorance *is* bliss."

The E.R.

Shortly after we arrived at the hospital, the emergency waiting room was bursting with neighbors and friends. How did they already know that we were at the hospital? Apparently, after that one phone call to my neighbors, word traveled fast that Mike was taken to the hospital.

The "angels in disguise" wrote their address and phone number on a scrap of paper, so I could call them the next day with an update. They could see I was well taken care of, so they quietly slipped out of the Emergency Room—just as quietly as they had slipped into my life. I never saw them again, but I did remember to call them the next day as I had promised. I will never forget their kindness to me on that cold February night in 1985.

Living the Movie Script

Within two hours, I was living the movie script of *Places in the Heart.* My thirty-seven-year-old healthy husband—who played racquet ball three times a week—was officially pronounced "dead on arrival" at the hospital. And what was the cause of death? How could he have been so alive one minute and be so dead the next minute, without showing any signs of distress? The ER doctor explained that it was a massive heart attack, likely due to ventricular fibrillation. He assured me that often there are no warning signs with this diagnosis. In fact, later I talked to a widow whose husband had just passed his annual physical (with flying colors), but as he was leaving he died on the steps of the doctor's office—due to ventricular fibrillation.

In the blink of an eye, my world was shattered and turned upside down. In the blink of an eye, our life together was over. In the blink of an eye, I was a 33-year-old widow. In the blink of an eye, I was a single parent with two young children. In the blink of an eye—just like Edna—now I was responsible for every detail of our lives . . . and I felt all alone, just like she portrayed in the movie.

Even in the ER—amidst a roomful of people who loved us—I felt all alone . . . and numb. It's hard to find words to describe that very moment. I couldn't grasp the reality of it all. Suddenly, without any warning, I was experiencing what had just happened in the movie. I was Edna. It wasn't during the Great Depression; it was 1985. It wasn't in Waxachie, Texas; it was in Roswell, Georgia. It wasn't a drive-by shooting; it was inside a movie theater. It wasn't the result of a gunshot wound; it was a massive heart attack. But just like Edna, I had no warning and I had two young children. In the blink of an eye, I was living the movie's storyline. What are the odds of that happening? Certainly, I'm a rare statistic in that category.

Throughout our celebration dinner that night, the idea of widowhood wasn't anywhere on my radar screen—at all. We had made it a practice to go out for a date night on Friday or Saturday nights, so it was a normal routine for us.

But on this particular night, it was a spontaneous decision. Like usual, we talked about the kids. We laughed a lot. Our conversation was peppered with highlights about his new clients. We talked about the Sunday School lesson he was going to teach that weekend. I have relived that dinner a thousand times, and there were absolutely no signs that Mike didn't feel well—none, not one.

Just two months earlier the cardiologist gave him a clean bill of health. He was checked annually, due to his family's history. Furthermore, Mike played racquet ball three times a week. He wasn't overweight. His bad knees kept him out of the military, but other than that he was healthy. So even when the paramedics were working on him at the theater, it never crossed my mind that it was anything serious.

"HAVE A GREAT NIGHT!"

As I left the Emergency Room that night, a teenage boy handed me a brown paper sandwich bag and enthusiastically said, "Have a great night!"

Did that kid really say that to me? Every fiber of my being wanted to shout, "Really? What do you mean, 'Have a great night?' Don't you know what's in this brown paper bag?" I clearly remember those thoughts racing through my head. His words were so insensitive at that defining moment in my life. I wanted to scream at that kid for his thoughtless words—and I'm not even a screamer! But

I was too numb and too weak to expend the energy to yell at him. I just stood there—perfectly silent and stunned. The contents in that brown paper bag consisted of my husband's wallet, watch and wedding ring. That was all I had left of him. I took the brown paper sandwich bag from the kid and walked out the ER door wondering, "Would I *ever* have another "great night?" My high school sweetheart, my best friend, my soft place to fall, the love of my life, the guy I had known since I was in the eighth grade, my husband, our children's father, the one who brought such joy and laughter into our lives . . . just died.

To this day—more than thirty years later—the brown paper bag incident is indelibly etched in my memory. *Every single time* I see a brown paper sandwich bag, it triggers that scene like it happened last night, and I hear those words echoing loud and clear,

"HAVE A GREAT NIGHT."

"HAVE A GREAT NIGHT."

"HAVE A GREAT NIGHT."

CHAPTER TWO

Daddy's with Jesus. Why Is Everybody Crying?

"Never be afraid to trust an unknown
future to a known God."
– Corrie Ten Boon

When I walked back into our house that night, the first thing I saw was Mike's sport coat and tie, hanging on one of the dining room chairs. In a strange sort of way, seeing his coat and tie brought a bit of comfort to me. That scene represented a tangible memory of his nightly routine. As soon as he got home from work, he'd take off his coat and tie and hang them on the back of a chair, so he was free to hug and/or wrestle with the kids. When they heard his TR6 come roaring up the driveway, they stopped whatever they were doing and ran to the back door to greet him, squealing, "Daddy's home! Daddy's home!"

I felt an undeniable warmth in my heart, but that initial moment of comfort was quickly replaced by a glimmer of reality—and I dissolved into tears once more. I tried, unsuccessfully, to wrap my head around the fact that I would *never* see that sweet scene again. The idea of *never* was too much for me to comprehend.

Our next-door neighbors took care of the babysitter logistics, so when I got home the kids were sleeping peacefully in their beds. The house seemed more quiet than normal. Huh. "Normal?" I wondered, "What does 'normal' even look like now?" Suddenly, there was no "normal." Life as we had always known it was gone . . . forever. I couldn't even begin to process how we would "do life"—without Daddy. Our children went to bed with a daddy and a mommy, but they would wake up with only their mommy. They had no idea that their daddy wouldn't be here in the morning to make our traditional "Saturday donut run." And then the truth of what happened hit me from another angle. In the morning, I had to tell them what happened. How in the world was I going to tell the kids that their daddy died, that he went to heaven last night? I was still trying to process the reality of it all, but in a few short hours I had to break the news to our children. But how, Lord Jesus, how?

"SOUTHERN TRADITIONS"

A dear friend spent that first night with me. She (a Southerner) warned me (a Midwesterner) that there would be people with food on my doorstep early the next morning. Apparently, I was about to experience Southern hospitality like I'd never seen it in the past seven years. In light of that news flash, she encouraged me to try to get some sleep—a thoughtful and wise suggestion . . . but a futile one.

When I got ready for bed, it was like I was watching someone else go through the nightly routine. As I brushed my teeth, I remember looking in the mirror, trying to grasp a thread of reality—but it escaped me. How could everything that happened tonight be true? How could I be a widow? It was hard for me to even *think* the word—let alone, *say* it. You're supposed to be old before you get that label, right? My mother wasn't even a widow—how could I be one?

It was all so surreal. In hindsight, it's almost comical that I actually thought I was going to sleep (that tells you the depth of my state of shock)! When I crawled into our bed my body was still numb, but my mind wouldn't stop racing . . . and our bed felt so very big and so very empty.

Needless to say, I didn't sleep. I relived every minute of the night—from dinner to the brown paper bag incident at the hospital. My mind was surprisingly alert, recalling every detail of the evening, while searching for some clue that I had missed—a clue that Mike didn't feel well at dinner or at the movie. I was desperate to make sure there wasn't some sign or symptom that I had overlooked during the evening. But no, there had been nothing abnormal. Mike was fine. It had been a great date night! Oh, that thought deepened the pain in my heart as a sliver of reality surfaced again—it was the *last* date night we would ever have.

After several rounds of replaying the details of dinner and the specific facts at the theater, my thoughts shifted once again to telling the kids. *How* was I going to tell our kids that Daddy didn't come home—that Daddy was in heaven? Even though I was there when it happened, I was still struggling to comprehend the reality of Mike's sudden death. How would I tell our eight-year-old son and our four-year-old daughter that Daddy was in heaven with Jesus? How could it be true that Daddy would never walk into our house again?

Since I didn't have any immediate answers to my questions, my mind raced to the future. Daddy would never coach another Little League game with Jay or see Julie perform another gymnastics routine. Never again would Daddy tuck them into bed, read them a Bible story, or pray with them. He wouldn't be there for their high school or college graduations . . . or for their weddings. He would never meet their spouses or know his future grandchildren. Our two young children were sleeping peacefully in their beds, and my thoughts had raced ahead several years into the future. My thoughts already had both of them married—with children!

I couldn't shut down my mind. It raced from one scenario to another, practicing different ways of *how* to tell them. There were no words to lessen the blow. I never did fall asleep, but the arrival of daylight brought with it the harsh reality—the events of last night were true. It wasn't some horrible dream, after all. Mike was in heaven . . . forever.

Just as my friend had predicted, people started to arrive at our house with food. The children were still asleep. I had to wake them up and tell them what happened last night.

WHIRLING AND SPINNING

My thoughts were whirling and spinning. You know, I had been to countless church retreats and women's conferences in my life, and not once did anyone talk about *how* to explain the concept of death to a young child. And furthermore, how could I offer any comfort to them when my own heart was shattered? I felt incredibly inept. I couldn't think of any way to somehow soften the shock of my words. The doorbell kept ringing. I knew I had to wake up our precious children and tell them what happened before any more people came to our house.

As I walked into Jay's room, I was still praying and still clueless about what to say. It was a phase in Jay's life when he and Daddy spent a lot of time together doing fun stuff—soccer, Cub Scouts, camping trips, basketball, Little

League Baseball and playing on our new Commodore 64 computer. Yes, back in the day that was new technology!

Sitting on the edge of his bed, I gently rubbed Jay's back to help him wake up. Bleary-eyed he mumbled, "Why did you wake me up, Mom?" Our kids weren't accustomed to me waking them up—ever—unless we had to be someplace. My philosophy was, "Let a sleeping child, sleep." I told Jay it was going to be a busy day, and I needed him to wake up so I could tell him something important. I stroked his hair for a few minutes, giving him time to be fully awake.

I was still wracking my brain for *how* to tell him— I had no words. But the very moment I opened my mouth to speak, the Lord graciously gave me this thought and I asked Jay, "Do you remember what Daddy has prayed every night after our Bible story time?" Without any hesitation at all, our little boy looked right into my eyes and said, "God doesn't make any mistakes."

Wow. Oh, thank You, Father, for bringing Mike's prayer to Jay's mind. I took a deep breath and said, "When I tell you what I'm about to tell you, you are going to think that God made His first BIG mistake . . . but we have to remember—God doesn't make any mistakes. He *can't.* He's God."

Tears started flowing down my face as I said, "Daddy went to heaven last night." With a scrunched-up look of confusion on his precious sleepy face, Jay said, "*My* daddy?" He was clarifying that it wasn't his grandpa—my daddy—that had died. "Yes, your daddy." I hugged him tightly as we both tried to grasp the reality of it all. It was a lot to process at any time of the day, but it was especially hard to comprehend as he was coming out of a deep sleep.

Unbeknownst to us, for the past six months God had been cementing a biblical truth in our hearts with these five words—*God doesn't make any mistakes.* They would become our anchor as we weathered this enormous storm in our lives.

Here's the backstory on this nightly prayer. In the past six months, every night Mike had prayed some variation of these words during our Bible story and prayer time with the kids:

> *"And we know, God, You don't make any mistakes.*
> *You're God. You can't make a mistake."*

Mike had started a new business venture. Capitalizing on his financial background, the business contacts he had made over the past six years in the Atlanta area, and his entrepreneurial skills, he had carved out a niche market that targeted small businesses. Home computers were a new phenomenon in the early 80's, and Mike's strategy was to help small businesses transition from the current mode of operation (green paper spreadsheets) to computer software. He believed the Lord had led him into this new chapter in his career—and his client base was steadily growing.

This prayer was Mike's way to help the kids understand God's sovereign care over the new business. He believed that God gave him the idea, God led him to this place, and that God would help him get the business he needed to provide for our family. Although Mike was praying these words in the context of his new business, God was carving the truth of His sovereignty into our hearts—night after night for six months. In hindsight, I realized that God's handprint was all over this nightly prayer.

HOW DO I TELL JULIE?

There was no doubt in anyone's mind that Julie was clearly "Daddy's little girl!" She "lit up" when he came home from work. As I walked into Julie's room, I was still wrestling with how to tell "Daddy's little girl" that she no longer had her daddy. I prayed all night long for wisdom about how to tell the kids what had happened, but there were no "magic" words for this news.

And furthermore, I couldn't expect Julie to understand what had happened. She hadn't even experienced the death of a dog or a cat or a guinea pig—or even a fish! All night long I wondered what her young mind would conjure up when I told her that Daddy died and he was in heaven with Jesus. I gently patted Julie's back to help her wake up, and her eyes slowly fluttered open. Like Jay, she was really confused that I woke her up. But when she heard all of the voices downstairs, in her sleepy morning voice she asked, "Why are people here?"

I told her that lots of our friends came to be with us today. She asked, "Why?" I took a deep breath and through my tears said, "Daddy died and went to heaven last night, and now He's with Jesus. Our friends knew that we would be sad—and they're sad too—so they came to see us."

I was not at all prepared for what happened next. She asked the following questions in "rapid-fire" fashion:

> "If Daddy's in heaven with Jesus, can we go be with Jesus too?"
>
> "Is anybody here for me to play with?"
>
> "I'm hungry. Can we have breakfast?"

It was proof positive that a four-year-old thinks in concrete terms. She didn't wait for me to answer any of her questions. Instead, she hopped out of bed to go get some breakfast and see if any of her friends were downstairs. But she stopped abruptly at the top step. The "wall-to-wall sea of faces" was a bit overwhelming for all of us. There were friends in our kitchen, living room, dining room and family room—before we had eaten breakfast. So, the three of us walked downstairs together.

WHY IS EVERYBODY CRYING?

The outpouring of love was only surpassed by the "shock factor"—as everyone was trying to grasp the reality of it all. Mike had just taught our adult Sunday School class six days before, and he was very much alive and well. In fact, his lesson centered around the following four statements:

"Jesus is Lord.

God is in control.

The victory is ours.

Life is tough."

Those four statements—Mike's last Sunday School lesson—left a powerful impact on us as it related to his sudden death. His words rang in my ears, and I would hang onto those truths. God wasn't surprised or taken off guard, but we certainly were.

People were coming and going all morning, and I was receiving a steady stream of phone calls from family and friends in Ohio and Indiana. For most of our friends this was the first experience of death with someone in our age bracket.

At some point (when I wasn't taking a phone call), it occurred to me that I hadn't seen the kids for a while. I opened the door to our laundry/toy room, where I saw Jay curled up in the corner by the pantry, sobbing—and Julie was standing beside him. I walked in just in time to see her little hand patting Jay's shoulder as she said, "Daddy's with Jesus and Jesus loves Daddy. Why *is* everybody crying?"

In the coming days, our little girl would teach me about what "childlike faith" looks like in everyday life. She was too young to grasp the "neverness" of death, but she knew lots of Bible stories and for the most part she accurately applied those biblical truths with her four-year-old reasoning skills. She had heard many times that Jesus was in heaven, so she knew heaven was a good place—and she naturally concluded that it was a good thing that Daddy was in heaven with Jesus.

A FIERY TRIAL

Once again, I went to bed—exhausted. The bed still felt just as big and empty and cold as the night before. Although I was emotionally, mentally, and physically drained—once again sleep escaped me, so I opened my Bible, hoping that reading would eventually lead me to a few hours of sleep. I stopped where I saw two verses I had underlined in 1 Peter:

> *"In this you greatly rejoice, even though now for a little while, if necessary, you have been distressed by various trials, that the proof of your faith, being more precious than gold, which is perishable, even though tested by fire, may be found to result in praise and glory and honor at the revelation of Jesus Christ"* (1 Peter 1:6-7 NASB).

I was definitely in a fiery trial, but it felt more like "an entire lifetime" kind of trial—not a "*for a little while*" kind of trial.

After dozing off and on during the rest of the night, morning arrived right on time—whether I was ready or not. We were off to Funeral #1. There aren't enough pages in this book to name the countless people who helped us during those early days. And no doubt, I'd forget somebody if I did attempt to name all of our treasured friends that came to our rescue. You know who you are, and I am forever grateful to each and every one of you who were there for us from the beginning . . . and you've continued to show up for years upon years.

CHAPTER THREE

One Funeral Down... and One to Go

> *"So, it's true when all is said and done,
> grief is the price we pay for love."*
> – E.A. Bucchianeri

We were surrounded with so many wonderful friends at Funeral #1 in Georgia. Because Mike had taught an adult Sunday School class for several years, there were many fond memories, funny stories and words of encouragement regarding the impact of his teaching and his life on others. I felt very blessed to have shared our lives with dear friends in those early years of our life in the South.

One of the most painful parts for all of us was watching Jay grieve. He was old enough to understand the permanence of death, and it was heart-wrenching to watch him cry his little heart out. At the same time, though, I was grateful he wasn't stuffing his feelings or attempting to put on a "game face." We left the church and headed to the Atlanta airport. A dear friend flew with us to Ohio. It was so helpful to have him make the trip with us—someone with a clear mind who could help with the many logistics of air travel …with two children and a distraught woman.

At Funeral #2, I was again comforted by family and long-time friends from Indiana and Ohio. Unfortunately, our trip North was extended for several days due to a severe snowstorm. After all, it was February in Ohio. The irony was classic. One of the reasons we loved Atlanta so much was the lack of snow during the winter months … and here we were stuck in Ohio—in a full-blown blizzard!

Some of our Indiana friends thought they could make it home, but shortly into the trip the visibility was so limited they had to pull off to the side of the road. Thankfully, a sheriff drove by and escorted them to the local police station—where they spent the night. It made for some great stories—spending the night in a jail on the way home from a funeral! Best of all, it provided some comic relief—which was a gift indeed! I don't know if this is biblically accurate, but I had an inkling that Mike enjoyed watching how this all played out—from heaven's vantage point!

"CAN WE SEE DADDY TODAY?"

Several days later, we finally got on a plane and returned to Georgia. After the initial "de-icing process" the flight was uneventful, except for a heart-wrenching question that Julie asked me. She looked out the window, saw the clouds below us and asked, "Can we see Daddy today? We're close to heaven, aren't we?" Oh, how I wished we could visit Daddy in heaven, but I said, "No, my sweet baby girl. The airplane can't drop us off in heaven today." Thankfully, she didn't press any further, but obviously the wheels were turning in her little head. I silently prayed, "Lord Jesus, help Julie. Help Jay. Help me. We are broken, and our hearts are hurting. Please give me Your wisdom to know what to say, what to do. Heal our wounded hearts. Help me to know how to help the kids live through our huge loss." Upon our descent into Atlanta the sun was shining brightly to welcome us home.

THE FIVE BEST THINGS TO SAY

After enduring two funerals with lots of well-meaning people, I feel obligated to share some practical suggestions about what to say—and more importantly—what *not* to say to a grieving widow.

1. The #1 best thing to say? *Nothing.*
Share your tears and give hugs, not necessarily words. Initially, the less you say the better because well intentioned words can be misconstrued, due to the widow's state of mind. Initially, nothing speaks louder than a heartfelt hug.

2. "Call me anytime—day or night—when you want to talk or cry with someone."

3. Share a happy memory or a great character quality about the deceased. Talk about them. Honor them. "What I appreciated most about _____ was _____." Generally, people go to great lengths to avoid even saying the deceased one's name. But most grieving families want to talk about their loved one. Plus, they are still trying to grasp the reality of it all.

4. "We'd like to have you over for dinner soon." Instead of taking food to their home, invite them to your house. The "empty chair" at the dinner table at home is a painful daily reminder for the whole family. Follow up in a week or two and suggest a specific day and time—and be willing to be flexible.

5. Offer to go to the grocery or run some errands for them. Again, follow up on your offer. The new widow may appear to be fully functioning, but she's actually living in a "foggy" world. Just to clarify, "grief fog" is a legitimate term in the context of grief. Confusion, forgetfulness, anxiety, and lack of concentration are all symptoms of grief stress, which results in the "foggy" condition. We put dinner in the oven and forget to

turn on the oven. We put frozen food in the pantry and cereal in the freezer. Once the person in grief is aware of the fog, it's like an invisible heavily-weighted shawl that envelopes our entire being . . . and it feels like the fog will never lift. Physically, we don't feel like eating, and we are sleep-deprived, so our energy level is depleted. Mentally, we are not thinking clearly because we can't put two thoughts together that make any sense. And emotionally, we are preoccupied with trying to make sense of our loss. So, it's an understatement to say that those in grief are functioning below their normal capacity.

THE FIFTEEN WORST THINGS YOU CAN SAY

1. "Call me if you need anything."
This might surprise you at first because it *seems* like the right thing to say. But here's the issue. Those in the early grips of grief don't know what they *need* or *want*. Instead, do one of the suggestions that was listed above in the *best* things to do.

2. "You know what they say—time heals all wounds."
Offering clichés can do more damage than good. At this point the grieving one can't imagine *anything* will heal her wounded heart. And in fact, time does *not* heal all wounds. Every celebration—birthdays, high school

graduations, college graduations, weddings—just rips those wounds wide open. The void left by the loved one who has died continues to be significant—years after the initial loss.

3. "At least you have the kids!"
In the situation where a spouse has died and there are young children, this statement *does not* bring comfort to the remaining parent. It's distressing—even terrifying—to anticipate the responsibility of suddenly being a single parent. There are also the adjustments of dealing with the children's ever-changing emotional needs. It's one thing for the adult to suffer and grieve, but it's an entirely different kind of pain to watch your children's hearts break—and not be able to "fix it" for them!

4. "You'll get over it eventually . . . give it some time."
Let's be clear, we don't "get *over* it," but we can learn how to "get *through* it." With God's help and time and faithful friends, we learn how to move on with our lives. The reality is, there are multiple kinds of loss that our friends face throughout life. Besides loss through death, there is emotional loss (damaged relationships), mental loss (destructive thoughts), physical loss (poor health), financial loss (bad investments), and spiritual loss (doubting your faith). The recovery time for any loss is an unknown variable, but may you be encour-

aged to "be there" for your friends—during whatever loss they are facing.

5. "Are you doing okay *now*?"
With loss through death, it's unrealistic to assume that everything is going to be okay in a few months.

6. "It's time to move on and start dating."
There is no set timetable for initiating a new relationship. However, it's wise for friends not to "go there" in conversation unless the one who has suffered the loss specifically asks for your opinion.

7. "You'll feel better when you get the insurance money and aren't worried about finances."
Be aware and sensitive to the fact that things aren't always as they seem. I knew of a family where the husband portrayed a "high roller" lifestyle. But, in reality, his wife knew they were in debt up to their ears. This comment was painful for his widow because there wasn't going to be any insurance money—only a boatload of debt.

8. "I can't believe you had a closed casket. I needed some closure."
Really? This grieving woman just lost her beloved spouse, and you're irritable about the closed casket? Best to deal with the "closure" issue in the privacy of your own home rather than criticize the widow's deci-

sion. In my case, we had discussed this very thing when Mike's father had died. The make-up job on his dad was done poorly, and he said to me, "If you're around when I die, make sure the casket is closed." So, the casket was closed.

9. "It's a blessing your kids are so young. They will hardly remember this."
Yes—those exact words were said to me. If that's all you've got, please don't say anything to the widow.

10. "All things work together for good . . ." Scripture verses were most meaningful when the Lord reminded me of His truth—not when a woman is standing there next to her husband, quoting that verse to me. Thankfully, I was able to hold my tongue!

11. "The holidays are sure going to be hard."
That was an understatement.

12. "Once you get through all of the 'firsts' this year, things will be better."
I wanted to ask, "How?" But I managed to bite my tongue and not respond.

13. "You should rent the movie you were watching to see how it ends."
What?! On multiple levels, I can't think of one reason I would want to do that.

14. "Don't worry about your children. Kids have an amazing ability to bounce back."
Hmm. "Did you lose a parent and 'bounce back?'" That's what I wanted to say, but again I used restraint and gritted my teeth.

15. "You're young. You'll be married in no time."
Maybe so, but it was *too soon* to make that suggestion to a brand-new widow.

Feel free to share these tips with your friends *before* they head to the funeral home. Hopefully, some future widows can be spared from words that only intensify their grief.

At some point, I started compiling this "ABC's of Grief" list. The left column describes the hopelessness I felt, and the right column expresses the hope I found in God's Word. It contrasts my feelings versus my faith. Maybe these truths will give others some hope, as well.

ABC'S OF GRIEF

A	**Amputee**	**Accept Help**
	(An integral part of my life is permanently missing.)	*"This is the message you have heard from the beginning that you should love one another"* (I John 3:11).
B	**Brokenhearted**	**Burden-bearer Is Jesus**
		"He heals the brokenhearted and binds up their wounds" (Ps. 147:3).

C	Crushed	Comfort in Jesus
		"The Lord is near to the broken-hearted and saves those who are crushed in spirit" (Ps. 34:18).
D	Dreams Shattered	Direction from Jesus
		"You will make known to me the path of life; in Your presence is fullness of joy; in Your right hand there are pleasures forever" (Ps. 16:11).
E	Emotionally Empty	Embrace God's Word
		"Guide me in your truth and teach me, for you are God my Savior, and my hope is in you all day long" (Ps. 25:5, NIV).
F	Fear	Faith
		"The LORD is for me; I will not fear; What can man do to me" (Ps. 118:6)?
G	Gut-wrenching Grief	Greater Grace
		"And God is able to make all grace abound to you, so that in all things at all times, having all that you need, you will abound in every good work" (2 Cor.9:8, NIV).

H	Hopelessness	Hope
		"Now she who is a widow indeed and who has been left alone, has fixed her hope on God and continues in entreaties and prayers night and day"(1 Tim 5:5).
I	Internal Turmoil	Intercession
		"He ever lives to make intercession for me"(Heb. 7:25).
J	Juggling Demands	Just Look to Jesus for Strength
		"Let endurance have its perfect result, so you may be complete, lacking in nothing"(James 1:4).
K	Kaleidoscope of Feelings	Know God's Character
		"The LORD will fight for you; you need only to be still"(Ex.14:14, NIV).
L	Lonely	Lord Is Near
		"The nearness of God is my good; I have made the Lord my refuge . . ." (Ps. 73:28).
M	Mourning	Mercy Magnified
		". . . for his compassions never fail. They are new every morning; great is your faithfulness" (Lam.3:22-23).
N	Numb and Needy	Nearness of God
		"I will never leave you nor forsake you"(Josh. 1:5, NIV).

O	Overwhelmed	Overcomer
		"In the world you will have tribulation, but take courage; I have overcome the world" (John 16:33).
P	Pain	Peace of God
		"And the peace of God, which surpasses all comprehension, shall guard your hearts and your minds in Christ Jesus"(Phil.4:7).
Q	Questions	Quiet Rest
		"Rest in the Lord and wait patiently for Him" (Ps. 37:7).
R	Raw Emotion	Run to God's Promises
		"He who dwells in the shelter of the Most High will abide in the shadow of the Almighty" (Ps. 91:1).
S	Suffering in Silence	Seek My Savior
		"I have set the Lord continually before me; because He is at my right hand, I will not be shaken" (Ps. 16:8).
T	Tears	Trust
		"In God, whose word I praise, In God I have put my trust; I shall not be afraid. What can mere man do to me" (Ps. 56:4).

U	Uncertainty	Unfailing Father
		"Seeing that His divine power has granted to us everything pertaining to life and godliness, through the true knowledge of Him who called us by His own glory and excellence"(2 Peter 1:3).
V	Voyage into the Unknown	Vessel of Honor
		"I have set the Lord continually before me; because He is at my right hand, I will not be shaken" (Ps 16:8).
W	Why?	Wisdom Needed
		"Will the clay say to the potter, 'What are you doing?' Or the thing you are making say, 'He has no hands?'" (Isaiah 45:9).
X	"X-Rayed"by All	"Xtreme" Adjustments
		"Cast your burden upon the Lord and He will sustain you; He will never allow the righteous to be shaken" (Ps. 55:22).
Y	Yearn for Yesterdays	Yield to God's Plan
		"Be still and know that I am God" (Ps. 46:10).
Z	Zig-Zag through Landmines	Zeal to End Well
		"A thousand years in your sight are like a day that has just gone by ... Teach us to number our days ... Satisfy us in the morning with yourunfailing love" (Ps. 90:4,12,14).

Chapter Four

Home Sweet Home

> *"When our faith intersects with God's will,*
> *extraordinary things happen."*
> – Andy Stanley

Facing a New Reality

After ten days of "non-stop grieving" with friends and family in Ohio, I didn't think my body could manufacture any more tears. But once again—I. Was. Wrong. Walking into our home triggered a new stream of sadness, and more tears flowed freely. I honestly hadn't anticipated this moment, but then I would soon find out there were *a lot* of things I hadn't anticipated. I wrongly assumed it would be a relief to be home. Instead, it brought new layers of reality to the surface.

Never again would Mike come home from work. Never again would I feel his arms wrapped around me. Never again would I hear his one-liners to make me laugh. No more times of sharing our hopes and dreams. No more date nights. No more vacations. No more parenting together. No more life as we had known it. That's it. That sums it up. Our life together as husband and wife was over—forever.

It was so hard for me to grasp these realities. My mind was flooded with questions. "How, Lord, am I ever going to be able to do everything?" "How are we going to live without Mike?" "Oh goodness. I have to find a job!" "What do I even want to do?" I was a Music Education major, but now as a single parent, I knew I didn't want to teach children all day long and then come home to my own children. Within minutes of walking through our front door, my mind was flooded with concerns and questions for which I had no answers.

In the midst of my own emotional roller coaster, it did my heart good to see how happy the kids were to be home—to be back in their familiar territory. The first thing Jay did was to go out to the backyard with a baseball and his glove. As soon as he started throwing the baseball, a great big smile covered his face. I hadn't seen even the slightest hint of a smile for over a week—and that was not typical for our easy-going, happy little boy. Julie had a big smile on her face too. She was so excited to be back home and play with her toys. Plus, she was getting plenty of attention and playtime from Grandma and Grandpa who had come to help me for a few weeks.

My emotions were reeling in a million directions, so I took my suitcase up to our bedroom to try to pull it together. But the first thing I saw on the dresser was the Valentine's Day card I had planned to give Mike. The outside of the card said, "What could be worse than Valentine's Day without chocolate?" The inside of the card said, "Valentine's Day without you."

Now you need to know that I'm a certified "chocoholic," so it was a *perfect* card when I bought it. But that was then. It was no longer a perfect card. I dissolved into a puddle of tears. Mom came upstairs and asked what she could do to help me. I couldn't get out any words to answer her. I just handed her the card . . . and then we cried together. Yes, I do love chocolate—but I loved Mike more.

FINDING A THREAD OF HOPE

That evening after the kids were tucked in, I opened my Bible—once again searching for some small thread of hope. Although I couldn't imagine that my shattered heart could ever fully recover, I needed some assurance that my Great Physician would somehow heal the enormous hole in my heart.

I turned to the book of Job. He knew first-hand about losses—multiple losses. Without any warning, in rapid succession Job lost all ten of his children and their spouses, all of his possessions, his friends and even his health. He lost *everything* but his spouse . . . and in hindsight Job probably wished God had taken her instead of his ten children! But I digress.

Through all of these mutual losses, Job's wife was less than encouraging. In fact, Mrs. Job suggested that he *"Curse God and die"* (Job 2:9 NASB). And to add insult to injury, his three "friends" threw out false accusations about Job. With a pathetic wife and no family or friends, Job truly experienced what it felt like to be all alone.

I found a small measure of comfort in knowing that at least I had both of our families and an abundance of friends supporting me as I entered this tunnel of grief. When I read Job's story, I stopped where I had previously underlined his response to these unimaginable circumstances:

> *"But He knows the way I take; when He has tried me, I shall come forth as gold. My foot has held fast to His path; I have kept His way and not turned aside. I have not departed from the command of His lips; I have treasured the words of His mouth more than my necessary food"*
> (Job 23:10-11 NASB).

Wow. In spite of all his losses, Job was determined to make his trials count for something. Those trials landed him in the "fiery furnace," and he *chose* to let the fire refine him . . . not just refined to silver, but to gold. Both verses indicate that suffering has the potential to refine us—to mold us into a new vessel, fit for the Master's use. Those words painted a powerful picture in my mind.

As I read the phrase, "*When He has tried me, I shall come forth as gold,*" it prompted me to dig a little deeper to find out what the gold-refining process was back in biblical times. Here's what I learned. Gold is a precious metal that cannot be manufactured. The goldsmith placed the raw material over a fire for it to melt from a solid form to a liquid form. As the impurities (the dross) of the metal rose to the top, the goldsmith would skim off the dross, look into the hot liquid and then turn up the heat. This routine was repeated until the goldsmith could see a clear reflection of himself when he looked into the hot liquid gold. At that point, he knew the gold was at its purest form.

The gold-refining process was a long procedure, as is the refining process in strengthening our faith. All of the information I read about refining gold eventually jogged my memory regarding a common poem that I had read on several sympathy cards.

The Refiner's Fire

He sat by a fire of sevenfold heat
As He watched the precious ore,
And closer He bent with a searching gaze,
As He heated it more and more.
He knew He had ore that could stand the test,
And He wanted the finest gold,

To mold as a crown for the King to wear,
Set with gems of a price untold.

So He laid our gold in the burning fire,
Though we fain would have said to Him, "Nay."
And He watched the dross that we had not seen
As it melted and passed away.

And the gold grew brighter and yet more bright,
But our eyes were so dim with tears.
As we saw the fire, not the Master's hand,
And questioned with anxious fears.

Yet our gold shone out with a richer glow
As it mirrored a Form above
That bent o'er the fire, though unseen by us,
With a look of ineffable love.

Can we think that it pleases His loving heart
To cause us a moment's pain?
Ah no, but He saw through the present cross
The bliss of eternal gain.

So He waited there with a watchful eye,
With a love that is strong and sure.
And His gold did not suffer a bit more heat
Than was needed to make it pure! (A.F. Ingler).
The parallel for us is that if we respond to our fiery

trials—faithfully trusting in our heavenly Father—there is the potential for others to see a clear reflection of God in how we trust Him in our time of suffering.

Another interesting facet about the refining process is that the goldsmith's hand never left the dial of the thermostat. Likewise, when we experience a fiery furnace episode in our lives, our heavenly Father never takes His hand off the thermostat. He has promised to never leave us: *"I'll never let you down, never walk off and leave you"* (Hebrews 13:5, The Message).

And one more thing—not only will He never leave us, but when our hearts are broken, Jesus weeps with us! In the story of Lazarus dying, when Jesus saw Mary and the others weeping, *"Jesus was deeply moved in spirit and was troubled . . . Jesus wept"* (John 11:33, 35, NASB). Think about that for a moment—our pain can cause the God of the universe to weep.

Something else I find to be remarkable in this story is that Jesus wept in sorrow for their hurting hearts, even though He knew He was going to raise Lazarus from the dead. Yes, Jesus hurts when we hurt—just like we as parents hurt when our children hurt.

JAY'S 9TH BIRTHDAY

And speaking of parents hurting when their children hurt—just nineteen days after Mike died, Jay had his 9th birthday. I couldn't imagine how we were going to pull off a birthday party, but it was the first of many celebrations that we managed to pull off. I was determined not to let our sorrow steal our joy! Since the Ohio snowstorm delayed our return trip, there were only a few days to plan his party. I knew I could get a cake made with a baseball theme, but that was about all I could manage, given all the other details I was juggling. Thankfully, "Mr. Bill" (our neighbor) came to the rescue. He was a "master networker" before networking was a thing! It just so happened that Bill knew Phil Niekro's neighbor, and Bill told that neighbor our story. The result? Seven little boys from Roswell, GA got to go to a baseball Hall of Famer's back yard and learn how to pitch "Knucksie's" famous knuckle ball! It doesn't get much better than that for a 9-year-old Braves fan . . . and the dads that went along were just as thrilled as the boys! They all came back to our house with lots of stories to tell while we ate birthday cake and ice cream. I made a "Baseball Diamond Cake" and decorated it accordingly to celebrate this special day. Thanks to Mr. Bill and Phil Niekro, Jay's 9th birthday became one of his most memorable birthdays of all time!

CHAPTER FIVE

The Many Faces of Grief

> *"The only person in history who did not deserve*
> *to suffer, suffered the most."*
> – John Piper

There are many faces of grief because grief comes to each of us, wrapped in a unique package. The answers to our who, what, when, where, and why questions vary when we compare our stories because our specific relationship to our loved one is unique. Furthermore, each of us is "wired" differently so it makes sense we would grieve differently. Some of the circumstances may be similar, but no two people have the exact same relationship because God created every individual to be "one of a kind." And that's another reason that there is not "a blueprint" to follow as each of us walks through the unknown in our own personal grief tunnel.

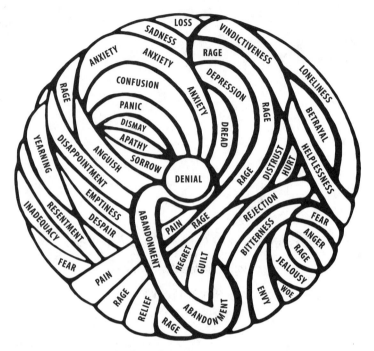

"Grief and Loss," Nathan K. Brendle Foundation

It's been said that "grief work is hard work." Whoever said that knew what they were talking about. In those early days of grief, it's difficult for a grieving person even to put one foot in front of the other—it's hard to walk when your entire body is numb. And it's next to impossible to function in your daily life when you are dragging around a heavy heart that's producing a steady stream of tears.

So, what about all of those tears? Let them flow. Understandably, grieving people need some time and space to cry. They're sad. Let them be sad. Sadness is part of the process of grieving, and tears are our body's release valve for stress, sadness, grief, anxiety, and frustration. Psychologists have suggested that all those tears have a unique healing power.

On the opposite end of the spectrum, we also experience tears of joy. Joyful tears have a cleansing effect and produce endorphins—our "feel-good" hormones. There have been numerous studies on the healing power of laughter and its effect on our psyche. The reality is, both tears and laughter come from the same deep well within each of us. Tears speak in every language—tears speak when there are no words.

The way our loved one died also affects which face of grief we will wear. Some have watched each passing moment as their loved one's body and/or mind disintegrated right before their eyes—their bodies becoming a mere shadow of their former selves. Others have lost their loved ones without any warning—and faced the shock of them being here one minute and gone the next.

I watched each of my parents dwindle away slowly, bit by bit. My husband, however, was gone in the blink of an eye. Both scenarios are painful—just different.

Some have correlated the loss of a spouse with the feeling of "not being whole anymore." It's almost like an amputee who "continually forgets that the limb isn't there, and then is crestfallen at each realization" (Lauren Fleshman). I believe that's an accurate description for grief. A vital part of what used to be our normal life is missing—and now, without our loved one, we no longer feel whole.

"I believe the hardest part of healing
after you've lost someone you love,
is to recover the 'you' that went away with them"
– (Chonda Pierce).

If you have experienced a loss, I'm fairly sure you can relate to the above statement. Most everyone you know wants you to "get back to being the way you used to be." People say things like, "Don't you think it's time to get over it and move on?" The problem is, losing a loved one is not something we "get over." Eventually (and the length of time is different for each of us), we will "get *through* it" and figure out how to make a "new normal" in our lives, but a "quick fix" to our grief is not to be found.

I heard a pastor say this on the radio one day, "The loss is irreplaceable and unbearable and unresolvable. The huge cloud of sorrow and grief casts shadows that block out any sunshine. But stop and listen. Hear the silence of God. We live in a broken world, in hopelessness and despair. The 'happily ever after' won't come until we see Jesus face to face. People want to hear about blessings—not shadows in the storms. Experience the pain. It's real. Job's story has no resolution for twenty-seven chapters" (author unknown).

Author Edgar Jackson gives an accurate heartfelt description of grief:

Grief is a young widow trying to raise her three children alone. Grief is the man so filled with shocked uncertainty and confusion that he strikes out at the nearest person. Grief is a mother walking daily to a nearby cemetery to stand quietly and alone a few minutes before going about the tasks of the day. She knows that part of her is in the cemetery, just as part of her is in her daily work. Grief is the silent, knife-like terror and sadness that comes a hundred times a day, when you start to speak to someone who is no longer there. Grief is the emptiness that comes when you eat alone after eating with another for many years. Grief is teaching yourself to go to bed without saying good night to the one who had died. Grief is the helpless wishing that things were different when you know they are not and never will be again. Grief is a whole cluster of adjustments, apprehensions, and uncertainties that strike life in its forward progress and make it difficult to redirect the energies of life – (Charles Swindoll, *Growing Strong*, p. 171).

I received so many cards with notes of encouragement that assured me of the prayers that were being lifted up to the Father on our behalf. There was one card, though, that so spoke to my heart I copied it in my journal: "There's an emptiness that can only be filled by our Lord, and more time and those of us who love you." Those words proved to be true for me.

GRIEF DOESN'T HAVE A TIME TABLE

Although our friends want us to be "back to normal" within a few months, it just doesn't work like that. Those who are grieving need time and space to be sad . . . to begin to heal.

> Against the backdrop of a quick-fix world that wants you to get on with life (mainly because your grief makes them uncomfortable), one friend told me, 'This is a long valley. People will give you weeks or months to recover. Give yourself a year at least. Maybe two. This is a wound God will help you manage. And you will occasionally bleed from it all your life, especially when you hear someone else's hard news. It will open that scar again—not to drag you back, but to move you to care for them' (*Letters to a Grieving Heart* by Billy Sprague, p. 25).

There isn't a switch to turn off our tears or a pill that will restore us to being "normal" again. And by the way, those in grief are trying to figure out what "normal" even looks like now. They have to create a "new normal" so please be patient with us. It's unknown territory.

It's also significant to remember that when you attempt to comfort your friends in their loss, talking about heaven doesn't magically make everything all better. The pain does not disappear just because we are assured that our loved one is in heaven. Eventually that truth does embody a good measure of comfort, but not initially.

It was ironic that many of the very same people who wanted me to "get over it and move on" just assumed I didn't want to be invited to any social event with married couples. At that stage in my life, most of our friends were married couples. So, one day I finally got up the nerve to broach the subject with one of my friends. I appreciated her honesty when she said, "We thought it would be hard for you to see all of us with our husbands when you didn't have one."

Oh. I guess that did make sense. I hadn't thought about it that way. They were trying their best to be sensitive to my situation. From my perspective, however, I wanted adults to talk to, and I needed to hear a man's point of view on things. I wanted them to invite me over when their husbands were home—not just when they were out of town. I missed hearing the logic that men bring to the conversation—but then I realized they didn't know that because I had never said anything. I was grateful that we all learned something from that conversation. The next time I had questions about why or why not my friends were doing something, I just needed to ask them. Everyone was trying to figure out how to navigate this unknown territory.

I heard the following quote at a retreat several years ago, but it was one of those sayings that stayed with me: "God will take care of *what* I go through. I must take care of *how* I go through it" (Mary Glynn Peeples).

Like so many things, we don't appreciate what we have until we no longer have it. I missed adult conversation. When I had a husband, I just took for granted hearing his views in our day-in and day-out conversations. As a widow, though, I soon realized how important it was for me to hear some logical thoughts from men—to counterbalance all the emotions that were pouring out of my women friends. Thankfully, we had been in a couples Bible study for seven years, so those guys and our neighbors gave regular input when I needed some logic sprinkled into the conversation.

ONE SIZE DOES NOT FIT ALL

When you walk through grief with a friend, she might seem fairly stable one moment, but then be in a pitiful heap the next moment. That seems to be the way it works. The grieving process is unique for each of us. One size does not fit all. We are all created with a broad range of emotions, and that was our Creator's plan—to create human beings as unique individuals. Our fingerprints are unique. Our relationships are unique. Our expectations are unique. Our responses are unique. Our habits are unique.

Stop for a minute and let that sink in. If you are reading this and you are the one experiencing grief, beware of those who want to "put you in a box" to comply with their preconceived ideas or timeframes regarding the grieving process. Remember, you are unique. And your relationship with your deceased loved one was also unique. So, you can expect that your grief won't fit neatly into someone's preconceived box. And that's okay. Like everything in life, until they walk through what you're walking through they won't—and can't—understand.

At the beginning of this chapter, I shared that I found a thread of hope in reading Job's story on that first night we were back home, in Atlanta. Let's look at Job's response when he lost everything but his life: *"Not once through all this did Job sin; not once did he blame God"* (Job 1:22, MSG). Job's response to his pain and suffering says a lot about his relationship to his heavenly Father. Job had lost everything—his family, his friends, his possessions, and his health. Take a moment and think about the enormity of those four categories. Or, you could create four personal lists to see what that would look like in your life—in black and white. Those four categories encompass a lot, especially in America in the 21st Century.

It occurred to me that maybe, just maybe, Job did not blame God because his relationship with his Father was deep enough for him to honestly question God—and then place his trust in Him . . . in spite of his own personal loss.

Up until I did this study on the gold-refining process, when I heard the word "gold" what came to my mind was a glittering, twinkling piece of fine jewelry—not a purifying process that took place under intense fire! As I pondered the refining process, I distinctly remember thinking, "God, silver would have been just fine! Did I really need to go for the gold?" But then, we don't get to choose, do we?

As I continued to learn more about the refining process, Job's story prompted me to make a conscious decision not to waste my sorrows. If I had to experience this heartache, I wanted it to count for eternity. I didn't know *how* to make that happen, but I knew *Who* would help me. A friend had said, "You know—many others have walked this path before you—but you are the first one of your friends to blaze this trail." Not only did I want to feel fully alive again, but I wanted to allow this fiery furnace experience to refine me into a vessel that was fit for the Master's use—a vessel that God could use to encourage others who would walk this path.

I memorized one of Elisabeth Elliot's quotes: "Pain is simply the difference between what is and what I want it to be." That about sums it up! Her husband, Jim Elliot, had been brutally murdered by the Auca Indians, the very ones for whom he had crossed the globe to share the story of the Gospel. Elisabeth knew how it felt to be in the fiery furnace of grief. Throughout the years, the godly wisdom she shared in her books gave me both comfort and hope. I also memorized the first sentence of a prayer she prayed daily: "I offer up today all that I am, all that I have, all that I do, and all that I suffer, to be Yours today and Yours forever." Her prayer continued:

> Give me grace, Lord, to do all that I know of Your holy will. Purify my heart, sanctify my thinking, correct my desires. Teach me, in all of today's work and trouble and joy, to respond with honest praise, simple trust, and instant obedience, that my life may be in truth a living sacrifice, by the power of Your Holy Spirit and in the name of Your Son Jesus Christ, my Master and my all. Amen.

The following words tumbled out of my heart one night when once again sleep escaped me, after a rough day:

WOUNDED AND BLEEDING

Wounded and bleeding from the inside out,
Crushed to the core, emotionally impaired.
Physically fragile and spiritually frail,
Grasping my faith by a thread so bare.

Wounded and bleeding from the inside out,
Defenseless and baffled by it all.
Too tired to know what I want or need,
Can't even think who to call.

Wounded and bleeding from the inside out,
The loss is more than this human can bear.
Broken and crushed to the very core,
The damage feels beyond repair.

Wounded and bleeding from the inside out,
My soul is desperate—trying to mend.
Exhausted from crying through sleepless nights,
It feels like the tears will never end.

Wounded and bleeding from the inside out,
Thoughtless words spoken bring despair.
Abandoned, defenseless and misunderstood,
Does anybody really care?

But then . . . gently I hear my Father say,
"You mustn't grieve as those who have no hope.
Through the storms I've promised peace,
Peace that passes all understanding, to help
    you cope."

"Come into My presence and give Me
    all your cares.
Take hold of My right hand—and trust Me.
I am your Rock, your Fortress, your Deliverer.
Come into My presence and find hope—
    in Me."

© 1985, Anne Alexander

ENCOURAGEMENT FROM
A NEW FRIEND

Details and more details bombarded me daily—transporting the kids to their extra-curricular activities, paying bills, dealing with legal issues, home maintenance matters, meals to fix, car repairs, insurance questions, house cleaning chores, choir rehearsals, and Bible study lessons. I needed a good dose of encouragement. I wanted some reassurance that my kids and I could not only survive, but thrive in the coming years. I didn't know anyone who was a widow with young children, so there was no one who understood what I was feeling.

That's exactly when a mutual friend introduced me to someone who had lost her husband ten years earlier. Her children were two and four years old when their daddy was suddenly killed in a work-related accident. The circumstances of her husband's death were different from my story, but the "shock factor" of our sudden losses were the same.

The first time we met, it was abundantly clear to me that her faith had remained strong—despite the pain in her heart. She was my living-proof example that it was possible to walk through this storm, depending on our heavenly Father each step of the way. Her kids were teenagers when we met—and they were "normal!" They both loved Jesus, in spite of losing their daddy at such a young age. That was my biggest prayer—that my kids would not reject Jesus because of the hurt in their little hearts.

What a gift from the Lord she was—and still is. I was like a "question machine" every time we got together. The more we talked the more I saw how she had allowed her fiery trial to strengthen her faith muscle. I'll be forever grateful for her consistent encouragement. Many years later the thought crossed my mind . . . maybe one day I could be that same support for someone. Was I willing and available to be used by God in the midst of this dark valley—whenever and wherever?

CHAPTER SIX

Never-Ending Daily Adjustments

"Faith is deliberate confidence in the character of God, whose ways you may not understand at the time." – Oswald Chambers

It seemed like there were a million and one decisions I needed to make and even more papers to shuffle. I soon came to regret those four words I uttered to Mike at dinner that Friday night, "Spare me the details." All of those financial details of his new business were completely off my radar screen—and it was fine with me if they stayed there. I had total confidence in Mike's business acumen, so in my mind there was no need for me to understand all those numbers when he began to explain some of the financial details to me. Little did I know how soon I would wish I had listened better to those "details." Thankfully, several of our friends helped me navigate through those murky financial waters.

Day after day there were new adjustments to make—things that I had taken for granted—like not being able to talk to Mike throughout the day. He had always worked locally, so he was available if a need should arise. We didn't talk that often during the workday, but just the idea that I *couldn't* talk to him was a bit unnerving. When an older widow (whose children were adults when her husband died) was asked about her hardest adjustment, her answer was, "The silence in the house." No longer did she have her mate to talk to, and the silence in their home was deafening. Because our children were so young, the "silence aspect" was not an issue for me—I just wanted to talk to an adult! I really did miss talking to Mike about so many day-to-day things. I've seen the following quote several places, and it perfectly describes my feelings—on more days than I can count.

"I wish heaven had a phone so I could hear your voice again. I thought of you today, but that is nothing new. I thought about you yesterday, and the days before too. I think of you in silence; I often speak your name. All I have are memories and photos in frames. Your memory is a keepsake, from which I'll never part. God has you in His arms and I have you in my heart" (lovethispic.com).

DADDY'S TOOTHBRUSH

Some friends had come to clean our house while we were in Ohio (yes, we had some amazing friends). But in cleaning one of our bathrooms, they threw Mike's toothbrush in the trashcan. I hadn't even noticed it, but since it was closer to Julie's eye-level, she saw it and she was clearly upset. She ran to me and anxiously asked, "Why didn't Daddy take his toothbrush to heaven? How will he brush his teeth every morning and every night?"

Now to get the full impact of this scenario, you need to know the rest of the story. She who was so very worried about Daddy's dental hygiene is the same little girl that made the task of brushing her own teeth a major battle—morning and night! The irony of it all was priceless.

FRAGILE HEARTS

Around dinnertime, Julie would regularly ask when Jesus was going to let Daddy come home to see us. She'd say, "Do you think Jesus will send Daddy home today? I want a hug. I miss Daddy, and I want him to come home now."

A mother's heart breaks when her children are hurting—especially when she is powerless to "fix it." Our love runs deeper than anyone can adequately express, and we want to protect our children from suffering, at any cost. I often reminded myself that if that's how strong our human love is, it's almost impossible to imagine how great God's love is for His children.

I believed with all my heart that God cared about Julie's four-year-old fragile heart, and He cared about what was going on in Jay's nine-year-old heart—and what was going on in my thirty-three-year-old heart, as well. He knew every emotion each of us was feeling. That being said, it was excruciating to watch our little girl—day after day—anticipate when Daddy would come home. Regardless of how many times I repeated that Daddy was going to stay in heaven now, she was adamant that one day soon Jesus would let Daddy come home to see us.

She could even verbalize her reasoning. It went like this: "Jesus loves me and He loves Daddy, and He knows I want to hug Daddy, so He'll let him come home to see me." She was one determined little girl, and she would not be deterred. Talk about feeling helpless. Eventually we tried a counselor for children that had been recommended to me . . . but she was unsuccessful in getting Julie to talk. After multiple attempts, I was advised to give Julie more time and try again later, so that was the new plan.

In many ways, Julie's four-year-old concrete thinking cushioned the initial blow for her—for about a year. However, shortly after she turned five, the reality slowly began to take root—Daddy might not ever walk into our house again. And that's when her tiny fragile heart broke wide open—one piece at a time. More times than I can count

I prayed, "Oh, heavenly Father, only You can mend our hearts. Please, Lord. It's so hard to trust You with the timing of it all."

On one of our beach trips, we went to the mall with our friends. We decided to stop in a bookstore and let all the kids buy a book to read. The kids all scattered to different sections of the store to look for a book. Julie was just beginning to read, but she quickly found a book she wanted me to buy. She slowly sounded out the words in the title as she handed me the book: *My Daddy Died and It's All God's Fault.* Hmmm. That got my undivided attention. I quickly flipped to the opening pages to see if I could discern where the author was going with this book. I found the explanation: the author had recounted her nine-year-old son's grieving process following his father's death, due to cancer. I bought the book. Even though the circumstances were completely different, it seemed to give Julie some measure of comfort that at least there was one other family on this earth whose daddy had died. In Julie's world, all her friends still had their daddies.

Who knew that a trip to a bookstore could end up being one of those painful moments that would blindside me? It was a comfort, though, to know that when we hurt, Jesus hurts with us. He cared about Jay's loss. He cared about Julie's loss. He cared about my loss. He cared about our friends' loss. I love how Ken Gire sums up this story in his book, *Windows of the Soul.*

Who's to say which is more incredible? A man who raises the dead or a God who weeps? Our pain can summon God's tears. He came to give hope to the hurting, lonely, sick, dying, abandoned, rejected, forgotten, ignored.

I found great comfort in knowing my pain could "summon God's tears." There were so many emotional triggers—different ones for each of us. Julie was so young she couldn't verbalize what she was feeling, and no one had ever been successful in getting her to reveal her innermost thoughts. No doubt, many of her random temper tantrums were a direct result of her hurting heart. It was the only way she knew how to express her feelings. Jay, however, would often just disappear into his room and stay there for a while. And me? There was rarely any forewarning when something triggered my emotions. As I stated earlier, a brown paper sandwich bag is still an "emotional trigger"—after thirty-plus years. Another "emotional trigger" for me is when I see a TR6 rolling down the road, with the top down—and in the South, it can happen year-round. My automatic response is to look to see who is driving it. Crazy, huh? Mike loved that little sports car . . . and so did I.

Hopefully, the following little chart will give you a dose of encouragement today.

YOU SAY . . . GOD SAYS

I can't figure it out.	I will direct your steps.	Proverbs 3:5-6
I'm too tired.	I will give you rest.	Matthew 11:28-30
It's impossible.	All things are possible.	Luke 18:27
Nobody really loves me.	I love you.	John 3:16
I can't forgive myself.	I forgive you.	Romans 8:1
It's not worth it.	It will be worth it.	Romans 8:28
I'm not smart enough.	I will give you wisdom.	1 Corinthians 1:30
I'm not able.	I am able.	2 Corinthians 9:8
I can't go on.	My grace is sufficient.	2 Corinthians 12:9
I can't do it.	You can do all things.	Philippians 4:13
I am afraid.	I have not given you fear.	2 Timothy 1:7
I feel all alone.	I will never leave you.	Hebrews 13:5
I am worried.	Cast all your cares on Me.	1 Peter 5:7
It seems impossible.	All things are possible.	Luke 18:27

(author unknown)

CHAPTER SEVEN

Can God Be Trusted? Really?

> *"God is most glorified in me when*
> *I am most satisfied in Him."*
> – John Piper

W hen we face a painful trial, we have a choice—
to be angry and bitter, or to choose to give that
anger and bitterness to God, asking for His peace and His
strength to "carry you" in the midst of the pain. It comes
down to this question: Can God really be trusted when everything seems so wrong? In order to believe that God can
really be trusted, we must determine if we are ready to accept that God is *who* He says He is. Is He really the Creator
of the universe? Did He literally "speak the world into being?" Did He create Adam from dust and Eve from one of
Adam's ribs? Did He determine the color of my skin? Did
He make my eyes green? Is He honestly the Lord of lords
and King of kings? Does God genuinely have our best in-

terests at heart—even when we are suffering and grieving? Until we've established who we believe God is, we cannot trust Him when painful and difficult circumstances enter our lives.

IS GOD OMNIPOTENT— ALL POWERFUL?

Genesis 1:1 says, *"In the beginning God created the heavens and the earth."* And the chapter continues with the repeated phrase, *"Then God said . . ."* God *spoke* the world into being. The Milky Way galaxy, alone, consists of billions of stars. "If you would count the stars in just the Milky Way—1 star per second—it would take 2,500 years to count them all. And the Milky Way is only one of hundreds of billions of galaxies in the known universe" (*Indescribable* DVD, Louie Giglio). God *spoke* hundreds of billions of galaxies into being.

> *Who will you compare Me to, or who is My equal... Look up and see: who created these? He brings out the starry host by number; He calls all of them by name. Because of His great power and strength, not one of them is missing* (Isaiah 40:25-26, HCSB).

Our Creator also demonstrated that He was all-powerful when He made man from a clump of dirt and woman from one of Adam's ribs. When God breathed the breath of life into some dust and a rib, just look at a few of the results.

Per day:

- The average human heart beats about 100,000 times. (That's nearly 2.5 billion times during a 66-year lifespan.)

- Our blood travels 12,000 miles.

- The heart pumps about 1 million barrels of blood in an average lifetime.

- Adults breathe an average of between 18,000-30,000 breaths.

- Adults exercise 7 million brain cells.

The medical world has come a long way in discovering many of the complexities of the human body, but there are still plenty of mysteries that confound the brightest of minds. God has created every human being on this earth, and each one of us is unique—fingerprints, dental imprints, and eye scans are all unique for every person ever born. No two human beings are alike. So, who am I to question the Almighty God, my Creator? *"Will the clay say to the Potter, 'What are You doing'"* (Isaiah 45:9 NASB)? Yes, I believe God is all-powerful, Omnipotent.

IS GOD OMNISCIENT— ALL KNOWING?

"He counts the stars and assigns each a name. Our Lord is great, with limitless strength; we'll never comprehend what He knows and does. He counts the number of the stars; He gives names to all of them" (Psalm 147:4, MSG).

God knows the names of every star in all the galaxies. If He knows the names of *all* the stars—stars that mankind hasn't even found yet—you can be sure He knows each name of every person walking on this earth. He knows us from the inside out . . . and He loves each and every one of us unconditionally. He knows when we feel strong, and He knows when we feel fragile. He knows when our hearts are broken, and He knows when our joy is over-flowing. To *know* that God is all-knowing and all-loving brings great comfort when my heart is hurting.

Our all-knowing heavenly Father also knows how many hairs are on every head of every person in the entire world. Yes, I believe that God is all knowing, Omniscient.

"He pays even greater attention to you, down to the last detail—even numbering the hairs on your head" (Matthew 10:30 MSG).

IS GOD OMNIPRESENT— ALL PRESENT?

"Where can I go from Your Spirit? Or where can I flee from Your presence? If I ascend to heaven, You are there; If I make my bed in Sheol, behold, You are there. If I take the wings of the dawn, If I dwell in the remotest part of the sea, Even there Your hand will lead me, And Your right hand will lay hold of me" (Psalm 139:7-10, NASB).

Not only is God all-powerful and all-knowing, He is all-present. God is available 24/7. When we're "emotionally broken," what we long for the most is peace. In the Greek language, "peace" means "to be bound together." What a perfect word picture! Since believers are bound together with Jesus, we can be assured that He is always with us in the midst of our joys and in the midst of our emotional or physical pain. It's hard to wrap our finite minds around this truth, but Jesus is "available" and "with us" day and night. He hears *all* of His children's prayers—at the same time, from every corner of the world. We can know, beyond the shadow of a doubt, that our heavenly Father is as close as the whisper of His name. He has promised that He will never leave us or forsake us (Hebrews 13:5, NASB). Yes, I believe that God is all-present, Omnipresent.

The truths that God is all-powerful, all-knowing, and all-present gave me both strength and hope in my darkest days. I wrote the following in my journal:

"Thank You, Lord, that I have the assurance that Mike is with You in heaven tonight. I still can't even believe it's true—so please let me feel one of Your heavenly hugs. You and I both know I can't do this alone. You know better than anyone else on earth that my heart is shattered into a million pieces . . . and only You can heal it. You also know that Mike truly was my best friend. The thought of living without him doesn't yet seem real. But thank You for bringing Scripture to my mind, even while I'm trying to grasp the reality that he is in heaven with You.

I've learned more about the attribute of Your sovereign care as I've studied the Bible. Now help me to transfer that head knowledge into a heart of acceptance. Isaiah 40:28-29 says, *"Do you not know? Have you not heard? The Everlasting God, the Lord, the Creator of the ends of the earth does not become weary or tired. His understanding is inscrutable. He gives strength to the weary and to him who lacks might, He increases power."* You are the only One who can bring comfort and healing to my weary body and broken heart.

Oh Father, already I want to give up and be in heaven too. My heart literally hurts right now—not only for my loss, but even more deeply for our children's broken hearts. I'm grieving for all three of us. They are so young. And the very thought that they won't know their father breaks my heart more than I can even express.

I don't know *how* we are going to make it, but I'm trusting You, Lord, to help us face our unknown future with courage. My confidence is in You. We are Your children and You love us. You are Omnipotent, Omniscient, and Omnipresent. When I reduce those big words to simple language—all-powerful, all-knowing, and all-present—those attributes describe a familiar phrase:

God Doesn't Make Any Mistakes!

Yes, Lord, I believe that You—God Almighty, Maker of heaven and earth—*can't* make a mistake! Psalm 46:10 says, *"Be still and know that I am God."* I'm asking for Your strength and Your wisdom and Your peace.

Then I read Isaiah 40:28-29: *"Do you not know? Have you not heard? The Everlasting God, the Lord, the Creator of the ends of the earth does not become weary or tired; His understanding is inscrutable. He gives strength to the weary, and to him who lacks might, He increases power."*

I have no idea what I am about to face in the coming days . . . and I'm guessing that's a good thing! Help me to remember that in Your timetable an entire lifetime is "a little while." After much rambling, this prayer could be summed up in one word—HELP!"

CHAPTER EIGHT

Keep Eternity's Perspective

"Thy will be done means my will be undone."
– Elisabeth Elliot

I clearly remember thinking I couldn't live another thirty or forty years on this earth with my broken and bleeding heart. And then I read, *"For momentary, light affliction is producing for us an eternal weight of glory far beyond all comparison"* (2 Corinthians 4:17, NASB). Hmm. That verse says that my pain on this earth is "momentary." It was hard for me to imagine the rest of my life as being "momentary" . . . but then, God operates on a different timetable. I guess compared to eternity, anything that happens here on earth is "momentary."

> *With the Lord one day is like a thousand years, and a thousand years like one day"* (2 Peter 3:8, NASB).

If I could try to see my new challenges against the backdrop of eternity, it just might make each day a bit more "doable." Maybe not to the degree of being "momentary," but at least I could try to adopt this idea of living with an eternal perspective. It gave me a glimmer of hope.

GLIMPSES OF THE BIG PICTURE

Soon after we returned home from Funeral #2, God was gracious to give me intermittent glimpses into His big picture. We lived in a small town—small enough that Mary was a neighbor to Sarah who worked with Ellen who was at the theater that Friday night. You get the picture. Through this web of small-town friendships, I heard many stories that confirmed God was using the circumstances of Mike's sudden death as a catalyst for some to question where they would spend eternity. I heard about a nurse who renewed her commitment to follow Jesus. She had done CPR on my husband at the theater, where she saw first-hand that "life is a vapor." God used his death that night to get her attention and draw her back to Himself. *"Yet you do not know what your life will be like tomorrow. You are just a vapor that appears for a little while and then vanishes away"* (James 4:14 NASB).

I also heard about a young man who made a public profession of faith that next Sunday at his church. He was at the theater that night, and he admitted that he was annoyed about not being able to finish the movie. But after he learned "that guy" died, he began to question where he would spend eternity. He wondered, "What if I suddenly died like that guy in the theater?" Not having an answer to that question prompted his decision two days later.

And there were several others who rededicated their lives to the Lord. Every story was a personal reminder for me to stay focused on eternity's perspective. Ultimately, heaven will reveal all the ways God worked in people's hearts that night on February 8, 1985—and beyond.

Another glimpse into the big picture happened to me one night when I was reading my Bible. For reasons unknown to me, I was drawn to the book of Isaiah, starting around chapter 40. I was finding consolation in Isaiah's words, so night after night I read a few chapters.

But those who hope in the Lord will renew their strength. They will soar on the wings like eagles; they will run and not grow weary; they will walk and not be faint (Isaiah 40:31, NIV).

"For the mountains may be removed and the hills may shake, but My lovingkindness will not be removed from you . . . And all your sons will be taught of the Lord; and the well-being of your sons will be great" (Isaiah 54:10, 13, NASB).

Isaiah's words gave me hope. As I anticipated my children's futures, Isaiah reminded me of God's love and His care for them. But here's when God showed me why I had been drawn to read the book of Isaiah. He had been preparing my heart with verses from Isaiah for two years.

I had been leading a Precept Bible study group for several years. In fact, I debated whether I should continue to lead a group because it was a significant time commitment. But I chose to continue leading a group because it kept me in God's Word—and if you are the leader, you can't "slack off" on your homework!

So, two years after Mike's death, I was leading a new group of women in the Sermon on the Mount study, which happened to be the same study that I had been leading at the time of Mike's death. It now became clear to me as to why I had been drawn to the book of Isaiah during those early days of grief. A large part of that particular week's lesson came from Isaiah, starting at chapter 40. God's handprint was evident. He had orchestrated the content of my study at that critical juncture in my life. I was unaware at the time, but God had been "preparing" me with His words of comfort. He knew what was coming—I didn't.

It took a few years for me to put the pieces of the puzzle together, but when I did, my heart was encouraged and strengthened to see how God had been planting His truth in my mind to strengthen my faith—ahead of my crisis and then again, after my crisis.

Behold, I have inscribed you in the palms of My hands (Isaiah 49:16, NASB).

It was still a moment by moment mental exercise for me to keep an eternal perspective—while dealing with the dailyness of life. If you have suffered a loss, you understand the "neverness" factor. Life as you've known it can never be the same. Every holiday, every tradition, every birthday, every place you've ever visited, every vacation, every friendship, every trip to the grocery store—every single thing about life changes, at the core of your being. Even when I recognized God's many handprints, my thoughts could readily dwell on what I *didn't* have, rather than on what I *did* have. When I gave into that mindset, my thought patterns quickly deteriorated into a negative "abyss." The following words flowed from my pen to describe the reality of that abyss. It's the "neverness" that is so haunting.

THE NEVERNESS OF GRIEF

As long as I still have my "earth suit,"
grief will be my companion;
It's different than other earthly trials that
have a beginning and an ending.
Grief has a beginning, but it won't end until
I see my Savior face to face.
That's it—that's why it's different.
It's the *neverness* that is so agonizing.

It can never be like it was . . .
it will never be like we planned!
Every holiday, every birthday, every
anniversary, every vacation,
Every graduation, every wedding, every
grandbaby, every major decision,
Every moment of any given day—
the *neverness* is there.

It takes on different forms,
but the *neverness* remains.
Sometimes it screams with intense pain,
raw pain, writhing pain;
At other times, it is a nagging ache.
Occasionally, it is so subtle that
life almost seems "normal."

But there is no "normal."
The dinner table has an empty chair.
The Little League team is missing a coach.
The gymnastics competition is missing a dad.

Only one car is parked in the garage.
A social security check is in the mailbox.
"Deceased" must be written on a
plethora of forms.
And on and on it goes.

An important person is missing;
Daddy is not here to share the joys . . .
Or the sorrows, the victories or the defeats.
There is no "normal."

One cycle of grief ends in time
for another to begin.
Oh—why can't it end?
Grief for the sudden loss of my husband . . .
Grief for my children's loss of their daddy . . .

Grief in watching my own father
become a shadow of himself.
More grief for my children's loss of their Grandpa.
Further grief in watching my mom
lose her battle with cancer.
And additional grief for my children's
loss of their Grandma.

The *neverness* of grief will continue—
because this earth is not our home.
But Lord, Your Word says . . .
You won't give me more than I can bear;
I'm not to be surprised by the fiery trials in life.

Your strength is made perfect in my weakness.
I am complete in You.

You will never leave me, nor forsake me.
Nothing can separate me from Your
all-encompassing love.

Only You can give me the peace that
passes all understanding.
Your mercies are new every morning;
Your grace is always greater than my need.
Life on this earth is a "blip in time"
compared to eternity.

GREAT IS YOUR FAITHFULNESS!

Yes, Lord—it's the *neverness* that is so painful.
But it's the *neverness* that sends me
running to my Strong Tower.
It's the *neverness* that strengthens
the roots of my faith.
It's the *neverness* that keeps me on my knees—
depending on You.

It's the *neverness* that allows the Potter
to re-mold this broken clay,
And that's Your goal and mine, Lord.
That this shattered clay pot be molded
into a new vessel,
A vessel that's *fit* for the Master's use.

© 1988, Anne Alexander

You, alone, Father, can transform the *neverness* I feel into a fit vessel—into a faith that can't be shaken—into an anchor of hope. Years later I read this quote by Dr. Idel Dreimer, "No mourning can heal the wound of neverness." It seems this feeling wasn't unique to me.

One Sunday the sermon was about the story of the feeding of the five thousand. "*Then He took the five loaves and the two fish, and looking up to heaven, He blessed them, and broke them, and kept giving them to the disciples to set before the people. And they all ate and were satisfied; and the broken pieces which they had left over were picked up, twelve baskets full* (Luke 9:16-17, NASB).

Jesus gave us a visual aid to show us a Kingdom principle:

> *Bread must be broken before it can be*
> *shared to feed the multitudes.*

Years after I had written *The Neverness of Grief* poem, I saw this quote:

> Grief never ends... But it changes. It's a passage, not a place to stay. Grief is not a sign of weakness, nor a lack of faith... It is the price of love.
>
> – Author Unknown

Thank You, Lord, that the *neverness* of grief is only temporary, in light of eternity. My time on this earthly walk is but a nanosecond compared to Your eternal timetable. Help me learn to *operate with eternity's perspective*. And it is in the choice to accept *"what is"* that I can find peace—in the midst of my grief.

IN ACCEPTANCE COMES PEACE

One of the phrases that Elisabeth Elliot lived by and often repeated in her writing is, "In acceptance comes peace." I had a choice. I had to ask myself, "Would I choose to *accept* my circumstances? Could I really believe in my heart what I knew in my head?" Intellectually, I knew that "GOD'S GOT THIS!" But my unspoken instinct was to see the remainder of my life as a marathon—not a sprint. That's what I was questioning—my ability to keep trusting over the long haul, not God's ability to keep providing.

> God wastes nothing. He weaves everything for His glory and our good. God doesn't waste our experiences; He weaves them for His purposes. (Author Unknown)

I understood my heavenly Father was offering me His peace as I entered this uncharted course for our family—uncharted to me, but not to Him. Although I had no idea about the next step to take, I knew in the depths of my heart that God loved Jay and Julie and me more than I could even imagine. I knew in my head that I could trust God; He already knew the end of our story, but I had to keep reminding myself because trusting was easier said than done.

That night I wrote in my journal: "Thank You, Lord, for Elisabeth Elliot's life and for her steadfast walk with You—in spite of the unimaginable circumstances she faced. I have learned so much from her books about *choosing* my attitude; she gives such practical advice. She says not to get so bogged down thinking about ALL you have to do— 'Just do the next thing.'"

Even with my "grief fog," I could remember those five words. The following quote from her encouraged me to keep putting one foot in front of the other:

> "From now on the life I live will be lived with no other explanation, but God Himself."

It was clear that *how* I responded to this life-changing trial would ultimately determine *who* I would become— not only on the rest of my earthly journey, but for all eternity. Each of us has to choose our response when the circumstances of life cause us to suffer. We can choose to become angry and bitter for the rest of our lives, or we can choose to accept whatever circumstances have been dealt to us—and find our strength and comfort in the *only* One who understands the depth of our pain. In order to weigh every trial against the backdrop of the cross, we need to look beyond what is seen to what is unseen.

The tricky part is that I could learn all kinds of Bible verses, but until they got from my head to my heart they really didn't change my outlook on life. I had to trust that my Creator—Redeemer—Father had not been caught off guard by my circumstances. That was the only way I could make any progress in the grieving process. Here are a couple of verses that encouraged my heart:

> *"Be anxious for nothing, but in everything by prayer and supplication with thanksgiving let your requests be made known to God. And the peace of God, which surpasses all comprehension, will guard your hearts and your minds in Christ Jesus"*
> (Philippians 4:6-7, NASB).

> *"The Lord's loving kindnesses indeed never cease, His compassions never fail. They are new every morning; great is Your faithfulness. 'The Lord is my portion,' says my soul, 'Therefore I have hope in Him'"*
> (Lamentations 3:22-24, NASB).

I wrote down the following prayer to remember:

> Thank You, Lord, that I can trust You to give me:
> Peace in the midst of pain,

Love in the midst of loss,
Serenity in the midst of sorrow,
Laughter in the midst of longing,
Discernment in the midst of distress,
Purpose in the midst of perplexity,
Memories in the midst of mourning,
Direction in the midst of disarray,
Mercy in the midst of misery,
Determination in the midst of doubt and
Grace in the midst of grief.

CHAPTER NINE

Take One Day at a Time

"Her absence is like the sky, spread over everything." – C.S. Lewis

Taking one day at a time came more easily at first because one day was all I could handle! Getting through one day was as far as I could think. But as the days turned into weeks, everyone expected me "to get back to normal." *Their* lives were "back to normal" so *my* life should be too. The only problem was, there was no "normal" in my life. There were so many more "not normal" moments than normal ones—and they slapped me in the face multiple times throughout any given day.

There were surprises upon surprises in this new life— too many to enumerate. It's not an exaggeration, though, to say that *all* the daily logistics of my life changed. One major adjustment for me was not having a second adult to help transport the kids to and from their activities. Just that one difference created a seismic shift in my life. Clearly, life as I had known it—my "normal" life—came to a screeching halt. I had taken for granted how much we shared responsibilities, until there was no more sharing—at all.

The "lonely factor" also loomed large. I felt so very alone—even when I was in a room full of people. One day I saw a poster that I bought and hung in the office, as a visual reminder that indeed I wasn't alone. The poster was a picture of a baby polar bear and it said: "Help me remember, Lord, that nothing's going to happen today that You and me can't handle together." I knew that was true—in my head—but it didn't always translate to my heart! That poster still hangs in my office—different office, but that poster conveys a significant truth I still need to remember each and every day.

My family and friends desperately *wanted* everything to be "back to normal" for me—and for them. But a "new normal" had to be established and I had no idea how long it would take, nor what that would even look like. In those early days, I considered it "a win" if the kids were dressed and fed—and made it to the bus in time!

The feelings of loneliness were magnified due to the "gazillion" decisions I had to make—decisions that would have long-term consequences for our future; decisions that I had very little knowledge about. There were several challenges that required me to seek wise counsel, but then there was the issue of where to find the best wise counsel. God promises that He will *"lead the blind by ways they have not known, along unfamiliar paths I will guide them; I will turn the darkness into light before them and make the rough places smooth. These are the things I will do; I will not forsake them"* (Isaiah 42:16, NIV).

In this verse, the descriptive words like "blind"—"unfamiliar paths"—"darkness"—"rough places" immediately jumped off the page when I read them. I honestly could relate to all of those descriptions. And then I read, *"So don't be anxious about tomorrow. God will take care of your tomorrow too. Live one day at a time"* (Matthew 6:34, TLB). I'm grateful that the Lord was faithful to supply wise counsel to guide me in all of those critical decisions.

The "grief fog" didn't allow me to plan very far ahead, and it forced me to *live one day at a time*. At the time, I thought I was functioning normally, but years later I've come to recognize that there are huge gaps of memory loss in those early years. Some long-time friends of mine met recently for lunch. While we were reminiscing, they were all remembering several events that I have absolutely no recollection of attending. Apparently, I was there in body—but not in mind! It's made me even more grateful that the kids and I all survived—in spite of my grief fog.

The Dailyness of Grief

There were many random surprises in those early days of learning how to cope. There were daily adjustments—

like seeing the empty chair at the table during mealtimes and sleeping alone at night. We had been married for nearly fourteen years and, in that time, I hadn't ever slept alone because Mike's work didn't require any travel. It was one of those adjustments that a widow has to figure out what a "new normal" will look like.

GROCERY TRIPS

Besides the nightly routine, another "daily thing" was feeding the kids. I know that probably doesn't seem noteworthy, but I didn't have an appetite for months, so I didn't feel like eating, let alone cooking. Thankfully, our friends' southern hospitality provided a steady stream of food for several weeks. I was so grateful, because the kids were hungry—and they needed to eat. My weekly grocery trips in those early days were largely for bread, milk and eggs; but on my first "real" grocery trip I had an extensive list. As I was unloading the final grocery items, the last thing I put on the conveyer belt was a head of cauliflower (fresh produce goes into the cart first and comes out of the cart last). Without any warning, the floodgates opened, and I began to sob. It was one of those "ugly cries." You are probably wondering why on earth cauliflower made me cry. Good question.

Well, you see, no one in our family—except Mike—ate cauliflower. I don't know why it didn't dawn on me when

I originally put the cauliflower into the grocery cart, but upon seeing it on the conveyer belt, I burst into tears and left the store—without my groceries! For those of you who don't know me, it's not typical for me to be so emotional—and certainly not to have a meltdown at the grocery store! But *nothing* was typical about my life at that point. It was just one of those unanticipated "reality checks."

No doubt when that young check-out girl got home from work that night, she relayed the story about her weird customer who left all of her groceries on the conveyer belt and walked out of the store—crying over cauliflower! It never occurred to me that going to the grocery would be one of the "daily things" that would cause me to grieve. The truth was, every meal—whether at home or away from home—was a stark reminder that Daddy was no longer with us.

"Donuts for Dads"

The school thought it was a good idea. On a designated day, before the elementary school-day started, dads and their kids ate donuts in the school cafeteria. It was an attempt to get the dads involved with their kids at school, since many of the moms were there to help in the classrooms throughout the week. It was intended to be a fun time for the dads to be with their kids at school—but what was meant to be fun had unintended consequences. Based on the low attendance, it was apparent that there were *many* kids who didn't have dads that could come and eat donuts during the week. Some dads traveled for work; other dads lived in a different city, and a smaller number didn't have a dad that still lived on the earth. Not to be deterred, the school continued to have a "Donuts for Dads" day in the spring.

The first year Julie experienced "Donuts for Dads" our neighbor offered to take her. Our kids and their kids grew up together, so she was perfectly happy to go with "Mr. Bill." When she got home, however, instead of her usual detailed "blow by blow" narrative of her day, she didn't say much about anything. She didn't have to. We both knew that it was hard for her. The next year she developed an "unidentifiable illness" on the morning of "Donuts for Dads." I let her skip school, and I skipped work. We got dressed and hopped in the car to get her favorite treat—donuts with sprinkles. We played all day! "Donuts for Dads" was one of those "daily things" that could be avoided, so we chose to avoid it.

There is plenty of pain in life that can't be avoided, so if we have the ability to lessen some of that pain, I feel we have an obligation to do so. Eventually, the school expanded the parameters to include aunts, uncles, grandparents, moms, dads, or a special friend. "Donuts for Dads" became "Donut Day" for the remainder of our elementary school days.

WEEK-ENDS

When Daddy was home on the week-ends, we regularly planned special outings that were filled with intentional family time. Now, however, week-ends weren't any different than every other day of the week—other than going to church. Since I was operating "on overload" anyway, there wasn't much energy left to plan extra activities. Thankfully, our friends were great about arranging fun things for all of us to do—or creating something to do for just the kids, so I could get a break.

HOLIDAYS & WEDDINGS

No matter what we were celebrating, Mike's absence was clearly felt—New Years, Valentine's Day, Easter, Fourth of July, Christmas, graduations, weddings. I'll never forget the first wedding I went to, alone. I "geared up" emotionally for re-living our wedding day, but I was not prepared for the floodgate of tears that erupted when I heard the words, "until death do us part." It's one thing to randomly hear those words at a wedding ceremony; it's another thing to have *lived* those words.

When it came time for our own children's weddings, I had everybody I knew praying that the joy of the moment would outweigh the sadness of their dad's absence. I certainly didn't want to spoil their special day and be crumpled up in some corner in a heap of tears! The Lord was faithful to help me hold it together, and I truly enjoyed both of their weddings. I'm sure it was because I had armies of people praying—from the East Coast to the West Coast—when each of them got married! As they grew older, one of my regular prayers for them was that they would make wise choices in their future mates. Thankfully, they both did make wise choices, so the "joy" outweighed the "sad."

Here's another handprint of God that was later revealed to me. For years I grieved over the fact that when Julie got married, she wouldn't have her daddy to walk her down the aisle. I never verbalized it to her, but it was an unspoken grief for me over the years. Every time I attended a wedding, it was a vivid reminder of Mike's absence to walk her down the aisle. But when that day came, I realized all of those years of my silent grieving were for naught. God had already been orchestrating a perfect plan.

Due to the fact that Julie's husband-to-be was stationed on the military base in Colorado Springs, CO, they got married in the midst of the beauty of the Red Rocks. There was no traditional aisle for Julie to walk down because her wedding took place outside. There was literally just enough space for the bride to walk around the curve of the rocks and meet up with the wedding party. She looked radiant in her white wedding gown against the backdrop of the Red Rocks and Colorado's clear blue sky. It was picture perfect, and I imagined her daddy with a great big grin on his face, watching from heaven!

ER Trips

In every family that suffers loss, there are "daily things" that are unique to that family's story. The fact that we had two young children with allergy-based asthma was a significant aspect of "dailyness" for me. We lived in Atlanta, GA where something is in bloom twelve months out of the year. The end-result was frequent trips to the ER at our local children's hospital—in the middle of the night—which required me to take both children, not just the sick one. I'll let your imagination paint the picture of how the next day went when we were *all* sleep-deprived—plus, one of us was on steroids! The positive aspect was that in the regularity of our trips we got to know the ER nurses quite well and they took good care of us.

Forms

Another "daily thing" that I certainly had not anticipated were the myriads of forms to be completed—schools, doctors, dentist, baseball, gymnastics, Cub Scouts, Brownies. Now, I was not new to filling out forms, so what made it so painful? On every single form, I had to write "deceased" rather than Mike's name. It was those kind of "daily things" that continued to rip open the wound of my ruptured heart.

BASEBALL

Our first baseball season without Daddy was another major adjustment—especially since Mike had always been one of the team's coaches. I remember telling Jay that he didn't have to feel like he needed to keep playing baseball just because he thought Daddy would want him to. I told him it was his decision. He could think about it and then just tell me when he decided what he wanted to do. Without any hesitation he said, "I want to keep playing, Mom. Daddy would want our lives to go on . . . and we can't change it anyway." In childlike faith, he "put the cookies on the lower shelf" and grasped the concept of God's sovereignty in one simple sentence—"We can't change it anyway." Now that was some wisdom from our 9-year-old! "You're right, son. We can't change it anyway! And I'm glad you want to keep playing. I love to see the grin on your face when you're playing baseball!"

MOVIES

One of my unique personal challenges was to actually walk into a movie theater again. I was fairly sure I couldn't avoid movie theaters the rest of my life, so sooner or later I would have to face the silent anguish that I had managed to evade. Remember, this was back in the day before Netflix or on-line streaming were options.

When a dear friend of mine from Ohio came with her kids to visit, we decided to go see ET—it seemed like a safe choice for my first re-entry into a theater. Plus, there was another adult available, if needed. I managed to make it through the initial hurdle of walking through the doors and sitting down in the theater, although I have no words to describe my emotions at that moment. In a split-second I relived the entire scene of the last time I had been in a theater. With God's help, somehow, I managed to keep it together. Thankfully, the kids were oblivious to me because they were so excited to see ET.

Everything was going along okay until ET received CPR and was revived. Without any warning, floods of tears silently gushed down my face. Why? Because that little alien creature was revived and brought back to life. However, when my husband received CPR, he was never revived. I felt a melt-down coming on, so I quickly left the theater to gather my composure. My friend stayed with the kids until the movie was over.

Emotions are impossible to predict when you are grieving. In the past thirty-plus years I've gone to lots of movies, without shedding a boatload of tears. But I have yet to enter a theater and not relive bits and pieces of that life-changing night in 1985. The venue left an indelible imprint on my heart that no amount of years can erase.

CHAPTER TEN

Find at Least One Blessing Each Day

"Broken things can become blessed things if
you let God do the mending."
– John Piper

WALKING THROUGH THE VALLEY

The Psalmist had it right when he reminded us of the necessity to walk through the valley of the shadow of death. Those in grief can't *go around* the valley! We must walk *through* that valley to get to the other side, where we can begin to create "a new normal."

The Psalms have powerful words to speak to a broken heart. One night I came across this verse, *"You have seen me tossing and turning through the night. You have collected all my tears and preserved them in your bottle! You have recorded every one in your book"* (Psalm 56:8, TLB).

The idea of putting our tears in a bottle is a foreign concept to most of us, but archaeologists have unearthed small bottles that were used by mourners to collect their tears. In ancient times, it was customary for those "tear bottles" to be deposited at the gravesite. The next time you find yourself drowning in tears, remember this age-old tradition. Take comfort in the fact that Jesus cares about you so much He has counted each and every one of your teardrops.

So how do we function in the midst of our brokenness? When there are turbulent and blustery storm clouds threatening to destroy any thread of hope, what can we do? One of my survival tactics was to look for at least one blessing each day. That practice helped me to focus on something good that I *had*, instead of being consumed with what I *didn't* have.

You see, my husband was "an eternal optimist." His cup was always half-full. Now I wouldn't say I'm a pessimist, but I'd put myself more in the category of a "realist." My first response is not to see the cup half-full or half-empty. I like to evaluate the pros and cons and then make my decision. But without Mike's daily optimistic perspective, I knew I needed to be proactive to keep a positive outlook as I navigated through this new maze of uncertainty. So, I began to *look for at least one blessing each day* . . . and I wrote it down. On one particularly dark day when I couldn't seem to find a blessing, I decided to tackle it from a different angle. I started to identify truths that I knew about God and turned those truths into blessings. I have pages of these blessings, but here's a small sampling:

What I Know About God, Especially When I Don't *Feel* It

- God is available 24/7—
  He doesn't slumber or sleep (Psalm 121:4).

- God rewards those who seek Him (Hebrews 11:6).

- Life on this earth is "a little while" compared to eternity (1 Peter 1:6).

- God's timetable is perfect because
  He doesn't make mistakes (Isaiah 45:5).

- God will supply my every need (Philippians 4:19).

God's truth is truth—whether I feel it or not. As I looked for a blessing each day, it became a habit that served me well. Why not consider starting your own list?

A Moment by Moment Choice

I was keenly aware that I couldn't always choose what happened *to* me, but I could choose what happened *in my heart*. It was a moment by moment choice. So, in my attempt to keep my heart right (on those days when everything seemed so wrong), I started to look for at least one blessing every day. It seemed like a tangible alternative to balance out the lack of Mike's optimism in the house.

Once I started down this path, I often found multiple blessings per day—which helped to cultivate a grateful heart. It is amazing how many blessings abound when we just get into the habit of looking for them—and some days I found them in the most unexpected places. Do you know what else I discovered? It's impossible to be grateful and have a pity party at the same time!

Some thirty years later Ann Vosburg has encouraged the same idea, urging her readers to "Start each day with a grateful heart" (*One Thousand Gifts*). Now I want to keep it real. I readily confess that there were multiple days when midnight was fast approaching, and I was wracking my brain to find a blessing for that day—even a teeny-tiny one. But the longer I thought through all the details of the day, God was always faithful to bring at least one blessing to my mind—every single day for the first two years of my new uncharted journey. As a by-product, this habit also gave me a measure of hope to face the next day.

After experiencing the positive effects of looking for a blessing each day, many years later I read an article by Alex Korb, a neuroscience researcher. He suggested four steps to take to achieve happiness, based on scientific data. When you "feel down:"

(1) Choose to be grateful—Ask, "What am I grateful for?" -Answering that question "affects your brain on a biological level. It activates the brain stem region that produces dopamine. It also boosts serotonin produc-

tion. And even if you can't find anything to be grateful for, it's the *searching* that counts!"

(2) Label the negative feelings—Ask, "What exactly am I feeling?"

- Put your feeling into just one or two words! Are you sad, anxious, lonely, prideful, angry, worried, feeling like a failure in some area, _____?

(3) Make that decision you've been postponing—Ask, "What am I waiting for?"

- Brain science confirms that "decision-making reduces worry and helps you solve problems because it calms the limbic system." And don't lose any sleep over questioning whether or not you made the right decision. "Perfectionism overwhelms your brain—it's stressful." In laymen's terms, he suggested that we just need to realize that "good enough is good enough!" It helps you feel more in control, which reduces your stress levels.

(4) Touch people—"Neuroscience has verified that humans have an emotional need to feel loved and accepted. One of the primary ways to release oxytocin is through touching—hugs, pats, handshakes." According to the neuroscientists' data, "touching someone you love has the ability to reduce pain."

So, if you live alone and hugs are few and far between, do the next best thing and call up a girlfriend and go to dinner. When you part ways, give her a good 'ole southern hug.

When we get into the habit of being grateful, it grows our faith muscle, which must be strengthened by being stretched. Have you ever thought about why David—as a teenager—believed he could take on Goliath? (Try to answer that question before you read any farther.)

David knew God was trustworthy because he had experienced God's protection and provision in the past. Remember when God gave him the strength to kill both a lion and a bear—without a weapon? He killed a lion and a bear with his bare hands! No wonder he was confident that God would help him take down the giant . . . with one small stone in his slingshot.

Take some time to encourage your own heart. Start a list to see how many blessings you can name—from your past to the present. As you recall God's blessings and provisions in your life, I promise you will find comfort and encouragement.

BLESSINGS AREN'T ALWAYS WRAPPED IN BOWS

As worship broke forth in my heart on this day,
I pondered God's greatness and powerful ways.

In wonder anew as I looked in His face,
I marveled once more at His wonderful grace.

All wise and unbounded, eternal is He,
He knows every pebble and shell in the sea.
The heavens and earth are His to command.
His sovereignty rules with a loving, strong hand.

His being is perfect and holy and pure.
He's righteous in judgment, unchanging and sure.
Yet mercy and patience flow freely in love,
I can't comprehend the Almighty above.

O why would He love us? We seldom obey.
We're sheep and we're stubborn; we want our own way.
He loves us in spite of our constant demands.
It's truly a mystery I can't understand.

His love knows no limit, His mercy abounds.
He gives to His sheep and the blessings are found.
Don't look for them only in gifts wrapped with bows,
But look in the hard things for you that He chose.

In sickness, in death, in heartache, in pain—
Where are the joys in life to claim?
Can you find the blessings, not wrapped in bows?
Yes. Jesus helps us conquer our foes!

His grace is unchanged. The blessings abound.
In His loving arms, peace is found.
He knows every thought, every feeling and care,
Just come to the Shepherd; He hears every prayer.

Now thanks be to God for He reigns above.
He's mighty in power and majesty and love.
His glory and honor we gladly proclaim,
The King of all kings, we will bow at His name.

© 1988, Anne Alexander

Speaking of blessings that aren't always wrapped in bows . . . one day when I was driving down the road I heard a new song by Garth Brooks. The context of the song was about a couple's break-up, but the phrase that spoke to my heart that day—in my context—became one of those "wow" moments for me. Garth sang, *I could have missed the pain, but I'd have had to miss the dance.* It had been five years since Mike died. Even though I had felt much pain, I was so grateful that I didn't miss the dance!

CHAPTER ELEVEN

One-Anothering

*"If you don't like your lot in life, put a
service station on it."*
– Corrie Ten Boon

When we find ourselves in hard circumstances we often fail to remember that people all around us are hurting. The more independent our culture becomes, the more isolated we are from one another. We pull our cars out of the garage, go to work, drive carpool, or run our errands, and then we drive into our garages and close the door. On any given day, more than likely some of us have little to no contact with our neighbors. They could be suffering physically, mentally, emotionally, or spiritually—for days or months—and we'd never know it.

Furthermore, when we are in the midst of suffering it is easy to believe some of the following lies:

1. **Lie:** If God really loved me, He wouldn't have let this happen.

   Truth: God loves you more than any human being is capable of loving you. His love is unconditional and eternal, regardless of your current circumstances.

2. **Lie:** No one understands. I'm beginning to feel like the "Lone Ranger."

   Truth: A lot of people are in pain. Look around. They're everywhere. It might be a different kind of pain, but nonetheless they are in pain.

3. **Lie:** I can't begin to face the future.

   Truth: You just need to get through one moment at a time, nothing more.

4. **Lie:** My world is shattered forever. I will never recover.

   Truth: Yes, recognize and identify your pain. You can't escape the reality of your suffering, but also consider the fact that humans do not naturally turn to God until there's some troublesome circumstance—something that we know we have zero control over. No wonder pain and suffering touch every one of us, at some point.

The most beautiful people we have known are those who have known defeat, known suffering, known struggle, known loss, and have found their way out of the depths. These persons have an appreciation, a sensitivity, and an understanding of life that fills them with compassion, gentleness, and a deep loving concern. Beautiful people do not just happen (Elizabeth Kubler Ros).

It's up to each of us to be proactive—to look for needs and then do what we can to meet those needs. And there's a bonus to meeting others' needs. When our focus is on someone else, we don't dwell so much on our own hurts and disappointments. One-anothering is not only the "neighborly" thing to do; it's the biblical thing to do. Approximately 260 verses (in the New American Standard Version) cover the topic of "one-anothering." Here is a random sampling:

"A new commandment I give to you, that you love one another, even as I have loved you, that you also love one another. By this all men will know that you are My disciples, if you have love for one another" (John 13:34-35, NASB).

"And be kind to one another, tender-hearted, forgiving each other, just as God in Christ also has forgiven you" (Ephesians 4:32, NASB).

"And whoever in the name of a disciple gives to one of these little ones even a cup of cold water to drink, truly I say to you, he shall not lose his reward" (Matthew 10:42, NASB).

"And that you esteem them very highly in love because of their work. Live in peace with one another" (1 Thessalonians 5:13, NASB).

One-anothering is about giving—and giving begins in the heart. Giving is the best way to fight off a pity party! Even while coping with the depths of grief, when we give to one another it not only encourages the receiver—it has a healing effect on the "giver." Giving people are others-focused; they go the extra mile to serve. We are never more like Jesus than when we give to one another. "The only ones among you who will really be happy are those who have sought and found how to serve" (Albert Schweitzer).

Giving is at the very heart of who Jesus is:

- He gave His life so that we who were dead in our sins might live.

- He gives forgiveness for our sins when we confess and repent.

- He gives strength to the weary.

- He gives comfort to the grieving.

- He gives unconditional love when our attitudes are unlovely.

- He gives promises that He always keeps.

- He gives grace that is beyond our need.

- He gives answers to our prayers.

- He gives us family and friends to love.

- He gives hope when we feel hopeless.

- He gives us opportunities to serve.

- He gives new mercies every morning.

- He gives good and perfect gifts.

- He gives wisdom from His Word.

- He gives peace that passes all understanding in difficult times.

- He gives unspeakable joy when we rest in Him (author unknown).

Jesus is the ultimate Giver of *all* things. Why not take a few moments and see what else you can add to this list? Then, evaluate your own "generosity factor." Consider how well you are reflecting the giving nature of Jesus in your day-to-day life. Every moment of every day, all of us have a choice to make—to live with a grateful heart for what we have or to wallow in self-pity as a victim, dwelling on what we don't have. Attitude is a choice. When we focus outward, rather than inward, it tends to change our perspective.

Do you remember the story of Shadrach, Meschach, and Abednego being thrown into the fiery furnace? I heard a pastor offer the following observation and I've never forgotten it: The *only* thing these three men lost in the fire was the thing that bound them—the ropes. Let that sink in for a moment. What might be binding you from serving others?

Honestly, I never even thought about widows—until I became one. I was widowed before my mom and before any of my friends, so I didn't have any frame of reference. Ultimately, that turned out to be a blessing; it caused me to turn to God's Word to figure out how to cope.

Through the years, the Lord has connected me to many widows to share His love with them—to "one-another" them as they walk through the many pitfalls of grief. My "fiery furnace" experience opened up an entirely new venue of ministry to young widows with small children—and now later in life to older widows as well. Let me encourage you to look around, find a need and *do something for somebody else!*

"BE STILL"

What comfort to have a dear Shepherd who cares,
As we give Him our pain, our sorrow He bears.
The Lord is our Shepherd; He will lead us each day.
Our job is to follow Him and listen to Him say . . .

Be still, My sheep, and know that I am God.
I alone can bring you comfort; take My staff
    and My rod.
This road of much sorrow I've walked in it too.
It led Me to Calvary where I suffered for you.

I know that your pain on this earth is intense,
But look to the future—heaven's glory is immense.
So trust Me each moment . . . one day at a time;
My grace is sufficient for each sheep of Mine.

Then back to our Shepherd we come for that hope;
We give Him the glory as we learn to cope.
Be still, My sheep, and know that I am God.
I am with you each moment, each step that you trod.

As you face each new day—may you "go for the gold."
I'm your dear Shepherd, to Me tightly hold.
Be thankful for family and friends each day—
They've been faithful to remember you and
    continue to pray.

Stand firm in the fact that I don't make mistakes.
Your days have been numbered —it wasn't left to fate.
Just look to eternity as you shine forth My light,
And soon that strong faith will become full sight.

"*Be still*, and know that I am God" (Psalm 46:10a).

© 1988, Anne Alexander

CHAPTER TWELVE

The Making of Gold

"When you can't understand His hand,
you must learn to trust His heart."
– Charles Spurgeon

Have you ever noticed that when God is working on your heart to impress a particular message, you begin to hear it from multiple sources? Suddenly, your preacher does a series on the topic, or someone posts a comment on Facebook that relates to it, or you hear a radio or TV preacher talk about it, or it's mentioned in your weekly Bible study.

After I had been prompted to study the concept of the gold refining process, it became one of those repeated topics for me. The explanation of the refining process was coupled with (1) teachings on God's power; (2) the hope of eternity; (3) the encouragement to live one day at a time; (4) the idea to look for a blessing each day; (5) and the concept that serving others results in a happy heart. Since the same messages were coming at me from various people and platforms—most of whom I didn't know personally—wisdom told me that I needed to pay attention.

Since I had been researching the gold-refining process, I took those biblical principles and created an acrostic with the word GOLD, based on Job 23:10—"*He knows the way I take and when He has tried me, I shall come forth as gold.*"

God Doesn't Make any Mistakes
Operate with Eternity's Perspective
Look for a Blessing Each Day
Do Something for Somebody Else

As I've shared these principles with people in various challenging circumstances, I've found that these action steps not only help those who are battling grief, but they are valuable in the midst of any difficult circumstance. The next time you come face to face with a hard situation in your life, why not overlay your trial with some GOLD? Or, if you know someone who is struggling, share this acrostic with them. It's easy to remember . . . and it works!

CHAPTER THIRTEEN

Peace That Passes All Understanding

*"Concentration is pinning down the four corners of
your mind until it is settled on what God wants."*
– Oswald Chambers

One day each of us will stand face to face with
Jesus. At that time, we won't claim any of the
titles we had in our various relationships on earth—wife,
husband, father, mother, daughter, son, brother, sister,
aunt, uncle, cousin, grandfather, widower, grandmother,
widow, friend, co-worker, mentor, or teacher. No, when
this life's journey is over we will stand face to face with our
Savior and Lord as His beloved child. On that day, the desire of my heart is to hear Him say, "Well Done."

"THAT'S FAITH"

To look into His face and hear, "Well Done."	- that's the goal
"To wait for Him in the unplanned place and to walk with Him at the unplanned pace" (John Piper)	- that's obedience
To give Him the broken pieces of my heart	- that's an acceptable sacrifice
To not get what I deserve	- that's mercy
To get what I don't deserve	- that's grace
To keep a quiet heart in the midst of life's stuff	- that's contentment
To release an offense	- that's forgiveness
To depend on God's character when I don't understand His hand	- that's trust
To keep an attitude of gratitude	- that's joy
To be totally satisfied in Him	- that glorifies God
To know that praise is my only hope for survival when I'm drowning in my circumstances	- that's worship
To renew my mind with God's truth	- that's peace
To remember that I will never need more than God can supply	- that's comfort
To have ears to hear and a heart to follow	- that's love
To seek wisdom to know what to do and to have the courage to do it	- that's courage
To take the next step when it is illogical, unfair, and not my way	- that's faith

© Anne Alexander, 1998

Until that day, God's Word says, *"Let the peace of Christ rule in your hearts"* (Colossians 3:15 NIV). Did you notice that little word, *"Let?"* It's a choice—to reject or receive our heavenly Father's peace, day in and day out.

> *"Peace I leave with you; my peace I give you . . . Do not let your hearts be troubled and do not be afraid"* (John 14:27 NIV).

> *"The peace of God, which transcends all understanding, will guard your hearts and minds in Christ Jesus"* (Philippians 4:7 NIV).

> *"You will keep in perfect peace those whose minds are steadfast, because they trust in you"* (Isaiah 26:3 NIV). The Message translates this same verse as: *"People with their minds set on you, you keep completely whole, steady on their feet, because they keep at it and don't quit."*

You might want to investigate some of the other verses that talk about appropriating God's peace. There is an entire "arsenal" of verses on the topic of peace—over 300! That's how important it is to God that we experience His peace, the peace that passes all understanding. There is peace in the present and hope in eternity to comfort our hurting hearts. Isaiah 41:13 says, *"For I am the LORD your*

God, who upholds your right hand, Who says to you, 'Do not fear, I will help you'" (NASB).

Minute by minute, hour by hour, and day by day we make choices that affect both our lives and the lives of those we love. So, here's the choice—to run *away* from God in anger or run *to* God for help. He really can give you peace in the midst of your pain. I love what Oswald Chambers said, "God does not give us overcoming life; He gives us life as we overcome."

The following words were written by Jim Wallis. I don't know his story, but no doubt he survived a difficult time at some point in his life.

> "The will of God will never take you
> Where the grace of God cannot keep you,
> Where the arms of God cannot support you,
> Where the riches of God cannot supply your needs,
> Where the power of God cannot endow you.
>
> The will of God will never take you,
> Where the wisdom of God cannot teach you,
> Where the spirit of God cannot work through you,
> Where the army of God cannot protect you,
> Where the hands of God cannot mold you.
>
> The will of God will never take you,
> Where the love of God cannot enfold you,

Where the mercies of God cannot sustain you,
Where the peace of God cannot calm your fears,
Where the authority of God cannot overrule for you.
The will of God will never take you,
Where the comfort of God cannot dry your tears,
Where the Word of God cannot feed you,
Where the miracles of God cannot be done for you,
Where the omnipresence of God cannot find you."

THE MYSTERY OF
UNANSWERED PRAYER

The Bible makes so many promises regarding prayer. The following verses seem to indicate that all we need to do is ask and believe—and our prayers will be answered to our liking.

Ask, and it will be given to you; seek, and you will find; knock, and it will be opened to you" (Matthew 7:7).

"Therefore, I say to you, all things for which you pray and ask, believe that you have received them, and they will be granted you" (Mark 11:24).

"For everyone who asks, receives; and he who seeks, finds; and to him who knocks, it will be opened" (Luke 11:10).

"If you ask Me anything in My name, I will do it" (John 14:14).

"Therefore, confess your sins to one another, and pray for one another so that you may be healed. The effective prayer of a righteous man can accomplish much" (James 5:16).

How can we reconcile these verses with our unanswered prayers? When hundreds of people pray about something and the outcome isn't what we prayed for—the prodigal child is still running, the marriage is over, the cancer spread into other vital organs—how can we still believe that God hears and answers our prayers?

Or what about those times when God's answer is "wait" and you are still waiting? There are also those times when God's answer is "No" and the story ends in death. These scenarios can easily tempt us to just stop praying because from our perspective, our prayers haven't been answered. But the truth is, we human beings have a limited perspective. There's more to our story that we can't see or imagine while we are still on this earth, but the rest of our story will be revealed in eternity. Until then, we have the ever-present Holy Spirit to guide us into all truth. He is our Comforter, the one who never leaves us nor forsakes us, as long as we journey on this earth.

God is the Creator of all things.

He is the Bread of Life, the Living Water.

He is the same yesterday, today and forever.

His mercies are new every morning.

His grace is always greater than my need.

His promises never fail.

His love is perfect.

His Word is truth.

He is more than able to handle anything
that comes my way.

He walks before me, behind me and beside me.

He is my hope, both sure and steadfast.

He is all-powerful, all-wise, and ever-present.

He shows no partiality.

He never sleeps nor slumbers.

He prays for you and me.

He comforts the brokenhearted.

He gives strength to the weary.

He remains faithful when I am faithless.

He offers the free gift of salvation.

He forgives and cleanses.

He is the Center of the universe.

He is the Source of all life.

He is from eternity past to eternity future.

He is the Author and Finisher of our faith.

His love will never be separated from me.

He is forever faithful, forever loving, forever strong.

He's coming again as the King of all kings.

And the list could go on and on and on . . .

The best is yet to come!

© Anne Alexander, 1998

CHAPTER FOURTEEN

God Is Always Working Behind the Scenes

"To wait for God in the unplanned
place of obedience, to walk with God at
the unplanned pace of obedience."
– John Piper

The moments turned into hours, the hours turned into days, the days turned into months, the months turned into years—and the kids had grown up. I was so grateful and equally proud for whom they had become as young adults. Jay now had a full-time job in the tech-world and Julie had a full-time job in commercial interior design. My constant prayer was that they would be productive, well-adjusted adults who knew and loved Jesus. Thanks so much, God! You answered my prayers above and beyond what I had asked, and now I continue to pray for them as they raise their own children.

Sometimes it takes a while before you see how God has been working behind the scenes, but oh how it encourages your heart when some things come to light. One day, Julie called me from work and asked me to keep Sunday, February 8, open on my calendar—because she was going to get baptized. She had deadlines to meet and couldn't talk anymore at that moment, but she promised to call me later with more details—which she did.

She had seen many baptisms through the years, but had never expressed any interest. I was anxious to hear what she would say in her baptism video. She opened with these words, "My dad died when I was four years old, and I've been mad at God ever since." Her words hung in mid-air in my head. I waited for what would come next. She continued, "But I'm here today to tell you that God has been faithful to me—no matter what!"

Have you ever felt hugged by God? This was one of those moments for me. Over all of those many years—behind the scenes—God had been mending Julie's four-year-old broken heart, bit by bit, year after year—in His way, in His time.

There's one more "handprint" from God in Julie's baptism story. It was a clear reminder to me of God's continued love and care for our family. In our mega church, baptisms are typically scheduled far out into the future, but there was one available slot the next week on Sunday, February 8.

Julie told me that initially she chose that date out of convenience because she had been asked to be in a couple of weddings in March. But before I said anything, she had realized the significance of the February date. The very *day* she got baptized was the very *date* of her daddy's death. Only God could have orchestrated that timing. Our loving heavenly Father gave us something to be joyful about on the exact date that had represented so much sorrow for the past nineteen years. These thirty-plus years later, the story still brings warmth to my heart and a smile to my face. Isn't that just like God, to eclipse our sorrow with a splash of joy?

A FEW OF MIKE'S
NUGGETS OF TRUTH

Mike taught an adult Sunday School class at our small church. Although he had taken some seminary classes when we lived in Indiana, he wasn't a preacher or a teacher by trade. He was an accountant. Above all, however, he believed the Bible was meant to be practical in our day-to-day life. One friend described Mike's teaching as, "He shares biblical principles that can be applied during Atlanta's rush-hour traffic on 285!"

Just a few months before he died, one Sunday morning Mike shared three simple words as the basis of his lesson: *KNOW – BE – DO.* He described these words as a "a roadmap" to maintain consistent growth in our relationship with Christ.

KNOW God's Word	Acknowledge with our mind
BE God's Word	Accept with our will
DO God's Word	Act with our hands and feet

To *know* God's Word takes time and it requires discipline. Unfortunately, time and discipline are two factors that most of us struggle with in our fast-paced life. We've been told about the many benefits of reading and meditating on God's Word every day. Yet, it's all too easy to rationalize getting some more shut-eye in the morning. And then one day of sleeping-in turns into a second and a third day. Before we know it, our good intentions go out the window and we fail to spend time with God in our daily routine.

When we do spend time in God's Word each day, we get to *know* God on a personal level. That's a great first step, but the next step is to choose to engage our will to *be* who He wants us to *be*. *Being* is a heart decision; it's when our will chooses to do the right thing. The last step in this three-part trilogy is to *do*—*doing* requires us to act on what we *know in our heads* and *believe in our hearts*. The physical action of *doing* involves time, effort and follow-through with our hands and feet. We can spend hours in

God's Word getting to *know* Who He is, growing in our personal relationship with God. And we can spend hours in repentance and praise to align our wills with God's will, *being* who He wants us to *be*. But the sequence isn't complete until we take our hands and our feet to act on our knowing and being—and actually *do* something.

So, how does this *know-be-do* concept work in my day-to-day life? Here's one example: I can *know* that God doesn't want me to lie—not even to tell "a tiny white lie." (By the way, there are no big or small lies with God; a lie is a lie.) I *know* that every time I'm tempted to lie about something, the *be* part of my will has a choice. I can rationalize that lying would be the easiest route and less embarrassing, or I can choose to resist the temptation to lie and *be* truthful because I *know* what God says about lying. Finally, I have a choice to *do* or *not do* what I *know* is God's will.

In the progression of the *Know – Be – Do* trilogy, first, we must get to *know* God—the all-powerful, all-knowing, all-present God. Secondly, the more we get to *know* Him, the more we desire to *be* who He wants us to *be*. As we practice *being* more and more like God—demonstrating His love, joy, peace, patience, kindness, goodness, gentleness and self-control in our daily lives—the natural progression is to *do* for others.

KNOW — BE — DO

These three simple words describe the essence of what it looks like for a Christian to successfully navigate through life. Hudson Taylor once said, "God's work done in God's way will never lack God's supply."

I ASKED FOR "SOMETHING SPECIAL"

In my ongoing quest to learn how to live one day at a time, the days, weeks, and months passed and before I knew it, Christmas catalogues filled our mailbox. As the kids were circling and underlining what they wanted for Christmas, the reality of it all began to sink in. "Uuuhhh, how on earth are we going to have a *Merry* Christmas?" Typically, I loved decorating every room in the house with a splash of Christmas décor. But this year, even the thought of putting up the Christmas tree seemed like a monumental feat.

Family and friends began to ask me what my plans were; I didn't have a clue. So, I adopted Scarlet O'Hara's mode of operation. I decided "to think about it tomorrow." I just couldn't face the reality of Christmas without Mike, at least not right now. It did get my attention, however, that I needed to start preparing—physically, mentally, emotionally, and spiritually. I began to ask the Lord to do something special—something amazing—during the upcoming Christmas season. I didn't have anything in mind. I couldn't even imagine what to ask Him for, but I knew I needed an extra measure of God's help and wisdom to carry me through this first Christmas—especially for the sake of the kids. I didn't want to be a "Debbie Downer," but the reality was, Christmas was going to be hard. Each of us had a huge hole in our hearts, a hole that would take much more time before we would heal. Emotions have many complicated layers. I had to keep reminding myself—I will never need more than God can supply! It became my "go to" thought when my emotions started to spiral downward.

I had begun the process of purging Mike's library, little by little. There were plenty of books to sort through—from accounting books to seminary-type books. So, I began organizing his books, stacking them according to the subject matter in the titles—not even opening the front covers. When I came to J.I. Packer's book entitled, *Knowing God*, for some unknown reason I flipped it open. I knew Mike had read this book, but we had never discussed it. I found the following words, written by Mike, on the inside front cover—dated May 15, 1982:

> Knowing God is impossible—'His thoughts are not my thoughts.' Knowing God is trusting Him in complete faith in all circumstances —particularly when it is illogical, unfair or not my way! Knowing God is accepting moment by moment what is, knowing that life itself is the true joy of that moment (considering all the given alternatives)! Ultimate knowledge of God is ultimate faith in Him—no matter what!

It made me laugh (which didn't happen much in those early months) to see how Mike interjected humor in the midst of this serious context. He wrote this note three years earlier, but what a treasure it was to find these words of encouragement—written in his handwriting—regarding his view of what it meant to "know" God. (I don't know why, but there's something comforting about seeing your loved one's handwriting.)

God had just answered my prayer of asking Him for "*something special*" this Christmas. It was a message I needed to embrace because Mike's sudden death was certainly "illogical, unfair and not my way!" This was another handprint of God, confirming to me that once again He had been silently working behind the scenes. It's been a gift I have treasured for all the Christmases that followed. It was as if Mike was saying, "You and the kids are going to be just fine because you know this truth about God— "*Ultimate knowledge of God is ultimate faith in Him— no matter what!*"

Mike

ABOUT THE AUTHOR

A nne Alexander grew up in Ohio in a loving, Christian family. She married her high-school sweetheart, and they lived in northern IN for seven years before moving to Atlanta, GA where she currently resides.

Anne became a young widow and a single mom when her husband suddenly died of a massive heart attack. She shares practical and spiritually uplifting insights to guide widows through the unique web of decisions that they face, a web that that continues to change as we age. Anne has had an ongoing ministry to widows for twenty-five years—through weekly small group Bible studies as well as individual church groups and women's conferences. Clearly, her heart for widows is unmistakable.